PRENTICE-HALL
FOUNDATIONS OF CATHOLIC THEOLOGY SERIES

THE IMAGE OF GOD IN CREATION, by Sister M. Charles Borromeo Muckenhirn, CSC

THE WORD MADE FLESH, by David J. Bowman, SJ

SACRAMENTS OF INITIATION, by Henry J. D'Aoust, OSB

THE ONE GOD, by Wilfrid F. Dewan, CSP

CHRIST'S REDEMPTIVE SACRIFICE, by William F. Hogan

SIGNS OF TRANSFORMATION IN CHRIST, by John H. Miller, CSC

THE ISRAEL OF GOD, by John M. Oesterreicher

SACRAMENTS OF HEALING AND OF VOCATION, by Paul F. Palmer, SJ

ESCHATOLOGY, by John J. Quinn

THE CHURCH OF CHRIST, by Maurice Bonaventure Schepers, OP

THE THREE PERSONS IN ONE GOD, by Gerard S. Sloyan

THE LIFE OF GRACE, by P. Gregory Stevens, OSB

FOUNDATIONS OF CATHOLIC THEOLOGY SERIES
Gerard S. Sloyan, *Editor*

SIGNS OF TRANSFORMATION IN CHRIST

JOHN H. MILLER, CSC

University of Notre Dame
South Bend, Indiana

PRENTICE-HALL, INC.
Englewood Cliffs, N.J.

Nihil obstat:

> Albert L. Schlitzer, CSC
> Censor Deputatus

Imprimi potest:

> Howard J. Kenna, CSC
> Provincial, Indiana Province

Imprimatur:

> ✠ Leo A. Pursley, DD
> Bishop of Fort Wayne-
> South Bend, Indiana

> March 30, 1963

PRENTICE-HALL INTERNATIONAL, INC., *London*
PRENTICE-HALL OF AUSTRALIA, PTY., LTD., *Sydney*
PRENTICE-HALL OF CANADA, LTD., *Toronto*
PRENTICE-HALL FRANCE S.A.R.L., *Paris*
PRENTICE-HALL OF INDIA PRIVATE LIMITED, *New Delhi*
PRENTICE-HALL OF JAPAN, INC., *Tokyo*
PRENTICE-HALL DE MEXICO, S.A., *Mexico City*

C

EDITOR'S NOTE

This series offers the depth and richness of the divine message of salvation proclaimed to us by Christ. The theology, or "faith seeking understanding," contained here is not on a catechetical level, nor yet on a complex, higher level; it is clear and nontechnical, but at the same time adult and thorough. It is a scholarly presentation of revelation.

These volumes do not adopt an apologetic approach. They neither attempt to justify Catholic faith nor aim at convincing those who do not profess it of the reasonableness of believing. This series is written primarily for those who already believe, who accept the Church as the living continuation of Christ, and the Scriptures as divinely inspired.

The authors do not attempt a philosophy of God or of Christianity, but a study of the mystery of God seen through the eyes of faith. The mystery of faith will not be dispelled by the study of these books. It will remain.

Since some background in philosophy on the part of the reader is needed, and cannot in every case be presumed, there are times when philosophical terms will need to be explained. Philosophical reasoning is very much a part of speculative theology.

Although the breakdown of the series is along traditional lines, each volume is designed to emphasize the oneness of God's plan of salvation and not its different facets. Distinction is made in order to unite. What is taught in the Scriptures is stressed, so that it may be seen how men of the Bible understood the message entrusted to them. The historical aspects of doctrine as held by Christians are then treated: the testimony of the early Christian writers and the liturgy to the belief of the Church; the controversies and heresies that necessitated defense and precise formulation, and finally, the magisterial teaching in each subject area. In this way speculative theology, or the present understanding of each mystery, is not seen in isolation from the sources of faith.

Thus, the revealed Christian message is viewed as the *tradition* (in the fullest and best sense of that theological term) expressed in and through the Church over the centuries—more explicitly formulated, from age to age, and with further applications. But it is still the same saving message begun in the Old Testament and perfected in the mystery and person of Jesus Christ.

One last point is important. Although the study of theology is an exercise of intellect, it can never be exclusively this. The message of Jesus Christ is a living Word, an invitation to participate in the saving event of the redemption, starting in this world by faith and the union of grace, and culminating in heaven by vision and immediate union. This invitation demands response or living faith. The study of the Christian message through theology requires such response, for the message is not something that was heard and assented to once. It is a Word addressed to us that requires our vigorous "Yes" for a lifetime.

CONTENTS

INTRODUCTION, *page 1*

CHAPTER ONE

"AND THE WORD WAS MADE FLESH," *page 5*

A story of signs. The fullness of revelation.
"Christ with us."

vii

CHAPTER TWO

"BROUGHT TO LIFE TOGETHER WITH CHRIST," *page 12*

Prodigal sons. "In the form of a slave." Victor over death. Two aspects of a unique mystery. "In Christ Jesus." The paschal mystery in the sacraments. "From glory to glory."

CHAPTER THREE

"MEDIATOR OF A NEW COVENANT," *page 26*

Eternal Redeemer. "A priest forever." "A lamb standing as if slain." Earthly form of a heavenly reality.

CHAPTER FOUR

"BY HIS SPIRIT WHO DWELLS IN YOU," *page 32*

The Spirit of Jesus. Christ raised by the Spirit. The Spirit of adoption.

CHAPTER FIVE

"SAUL, WHY DO YOU PERSECUTE ME?" *page 40*

*The body. "Of his fullness." The Church
as sacrament. The Church as mother.*

CHAPTER SIX

"SEALED WITH THE SPIRIT," *page 49*

*"Behind the veil." Sphragís. Seal of the
covenant. Participation in Christ's priesthood. A structured Church.*

CHAPTER SEVEN

"HE WHO BELIEVES IN ME SHALL LIVE," *page 62*

*"If Christ be not risen." "Come to me that
you may have life." "Unless the Father
draw him." Toward the unity of faith.
"One Lord, one faith, one baptism." "I am
the Bread of Life." "Sacraments of faith."*

CHAPTER EIGHT

"LIVING TO MAKE INTERCESSION FOR US," *page 75*

"I am the way." Imitations of the sacra-
ments. "Ask the Father in my name." A
mystery of togetherness. A family meal.
"Until he comes." "Reflecting the glory of
the Lord."

SELECTED READINGS, *page 103*

ABBREVIATIONS, *page 113*

INDEX, *page 115*

INTRODUCTION

God's word is not primarily something to be known. Neither is our human response to it exhausted by a mere assent of the intellect. For God's word, in its total complex, is not merely spoken; it is an *event*. It is the Christ-event.

To be sure, God has spoken much to mankind by way of instruction, but his revelation is always to be understood in the framework of a call, an invitation, an importuning summons. It would be a capital mistake to look upon the Bible and the volume upon volume of Christian theology as destined only for the enlightenment of the human mind. Pagan philosophers can do that. Christianity is much more than a doctrine. It is a life.

All revelation is summed up in Christ. The New Testament writers and the Fathers of the Church look upon revelation as rectilinear, as pointing to and consummated in Christ. In fact, St. John's gospel begins with the declaration that God's revelation has, in some sense, already come to term: "In the beginning was the Word, and the Word was with God, and the Word was God. . . . And the Word was made flesh and dwelt amongst us." God's revelation in the Old Testament was meant as a preparation for the coming of God's Word in person. The greater part of Christ's public life was spent in preaching the advent of his Father's kingdom, speaking words to prepare his hearers to receive the Word. Only after he had conditioned men to know what God wanted to do with them did Christ, the Word made flesh, uncover the fullness of his Father's word in the paschal event, the transformation of humanity in grace.

Yes, God's word is, in its fullness, a salvation-history. It is the living drama of God's entry into human history to recreate man in an ever more beautiful likeness to himself, to reshape man's twisted figure into that of a sharer of the divine life, through Christ. "To as many as received him he gave the power of becoming sons of God." (Jn 1,12) God's word spoken throughout human history was precisely his invitation to men to enter into a most intimate relationship with himself. God's dealings with his "darling Israel" were intended to lead men gradually to complete union with himself as his adoptive sons in Jesus Christ.

It is important to recall that Christianity is in no sense a dream about some utopian higher life for men. It is the divinization of mankind. "If anyone love me, he will keep my word, and my Father will love him, and we will come and make our abode with him." (Jn 14,23) Jesus Christ, then, as God's word in person, is spoken to us by the Father to call us to live the life of God in him. This God in whose life we have a share is triune, and so the living will be done in union with the Three.

Just as all revelation has been given to man to introduce him, through Christ, to the great mystery of God's life, so all theology—our attempt to understand what God has spoken—is designed to lead us to a deeper living of God's proffered life. This is the role of the sacraments, those sacred signs that comprise the subject of this book: to produce God's life in us, or, more in context of the revelation made, to reproduce Christ's life in us.

As God's word is a living word, so theology should be a living experience, leading us to commit ourselves to the Christ-life with our whole being. If we study the sacraments, through which this life comes to us, it is not because they are things of curiosity, but because they are the fundamental realities of the Christian experience. As God's word *done* through Christ, they are the unique source of our salvation and sanctification. They alone make us like to Christ, God's only Son; they alone make us over into Christ, for they alone make us participate in his life.

The sacraments are nothing less than prolongations of the incarnation which reproduce within us the paschal mystery, and that is exactly the way we shall view them. They accomplish this divine work in us precisely as actions of Christ through the operation of his Spirit in his mystical self, the Church, by means of the power of priesthood. This Holy Spirit is effective in all who through faith welcome him and receive him into their hearts.

CHAPTER ONE

"AND THE WORD WAS MADE FLESH"

—Jn 1,14

The incarnation is not just a truth of theology. It is a fact of human history. Because of it, the world and man have not been the same since. For the incarnation was not like a political or sports event that is over and done with as soon as it happens —even though it may be viewed by millions over television. No matter how lively the means, contemporary reporting methods merely record an event of the past; they cannot bring it to pass again. The Word incarnate does not belong to bygone ages in this sensè. God's incarnation is vitally continued and prolonged in the sacraments today.

We often say that sacraments are external signs of grace. This is true, but not in the sense that a flashing red light indicates the human message of either danger or emergency; or that a frown betrays a person's inner anxiety or anger. True, these signs express an inner reality in the order of spirit. The sacraments, however, express a supernatural reality. Other human signs not only signify invisible interior movements of the soul but also produce something new. The signing of a contract not only shows the disposition to agree about something; it produces that agreement in such a way that a new bond exists between the signers. A gift not only symbolizes friendship, but also solidifies that union. The sacraments go further; they produce the supernatural transaction which they signify. In this way they are rooted in Christ.

Christ is the first of all sacraments: he is the sacrament of the Father. As the Word incarnate, he clothes in visible, tangible form and shape the unseen and transcendent God. But he does not do this in a static or statue-like fashion; rather he is the dynamic embodiment of the living and life-giving God. Incredible though it may seem, the hypostatic union means precisely that the Son of God in person unites to himself a real human nature, our human nature, in order, in it and through it, to pervade and transform all human beings with the power and glory of his divinity. Through the incarnation, Christ's humanity becomes the direct personal instrument of God the Father's eternal plan to redeem men. Christ is God's revelation of himself, of his power, his love, his life—in person. The Lord Jesus is the sacrament of God in the most perfect sense. It was in the Word made flesh that "we saw His glory—the glory of the only-begotten Son of the Father—full of grace and truth." (Jn 1,14)

A STORY OF SIGNS

The day on which Mary conceived the Son of God in her womb was not the first time that God unveiled himself to man. The author of Hebrews says, "God, who at sundry times and in diverse manners spoke in times past to the fathers by the prophets, last of all in these days, has spoken to us by His Son. . . ." (Heb 1,1f) The incarnation of the Son of God was the climax of a long, slow, almost painful process for man in which God gradually unfolded the tremendous mystery of his life and love that he called man to share. The history of Israel is an account of God's successively fuller manifestation of himself to his creature, his "offspring." (Os 11,1) Not that God told men *truths* about himself. He could hardly have done this to early, ignorant man. God normally spoke through *action*, by means of some impressive show of his power on behalf of his people. As a result, they always thought of God with a vivid awareness that he was a *mighty*, living God. In fact, the first name for God that we find used in the Scriptures is *Elohim,* a word meaning sovereign power—a *plural* word, at that, indicating not just power, but the fullest concentration of power. Later, when God reveals his proper name to Moses, what does he call himself? He does not speak of himself in terms of an abstract attribute. Rather, he says his name is *Yahweh*— "I am who I am!" To the followers of Moses this could mean only one thing: that God was the mighty, living One who makes all things exist, the almighty One who holds the reins of the destiny of all nations and makes all events happen.

As the story of man unfolds in the Bible we hear the voice of God as he walks in paradise. (Gn 3,8) When it comes to ridding the earth of wicked men, God does not annihilate man in a moment. He sends the great flood, something visible and tangible, by which man can see God's great power and never forget it. (Gn 6,7) When God strikes a covenant with Noa after the flood, he gives to him and his posterity a sign of that covenant, the rainbow in the clouds. (Gn 9,12–17)

God appears to Moses in the burning bush. (Ex 3,2ff) The Almighty performs signs through the hand of Moses when he speaks with Pharao; so wonderful were they that even the Egyptian magicians had to admit that "Here is the finger of God." (Ex 8,19) Once Pharao had given the Israelites permission to leave his land, God was palpably close to his people in the cloud by day and the column of fire by night. (Ex 13,21f) As Moses approached the Red Sea with his people, God instructed him to stretch forth his rod over the waters. When he did so God divided the waters with a strong and burning wind. Once across the sea, Moses repeated his action, and the waters came tumbling down on the pursuing Egyptian army. God was thereby glorified once again; 7

his mighty hand had fought for his people, and the people saw his great wonders. (Ex 14,13–31)

God fed his people in the desert (Ex 16,12–18; 17,5f); he brought them to the foot of Mt. Sinai where his presence was shown in the fire and smoke and cloud covering the mountain top (Ex 19,16–19; 20,18ff); he even displayed to Moses some sort of corporeal representation of himself, not his face but his "back parts." (Ex 33,18–23) When, finally, Moses descended from the mountain, his own face sent forth rays of light as a result of his seeing and conversing with the Lord. (Ex 34,29) As God sent his people on their way to the promised land, he swore that he would defeat all their enemies (Ex 33,2), a promise that he kept through successive generations even after they had taken possession of Chanaan.

Many more examples could be given; the fact and manner of God's self-revelation, however, remain the same. He speaks to men through earthly images, actions, and events. All these are the signs of his hidden yet communicated presence and reality. Doctrinal statements about him come only later to explain who he is and what he has done for man. God's word of revelation is, first and foremost, an event that affects and changes man, and that event, for all its gradual unfolding, finds its fulfillment and completion in God's Word in person, the God-man.

The remarkable thing about all these manifestations to the Old Testament Israelites was that this very intervention of Yahweh, the living God, made of this group of nomadic tribes a *people*. They became God's own people, on whom he doted, for whom he fought, whom he chastised, and in whose midst he dwelt. This people Israel was God's "darling." She enjoyed such a special and powerful presence of the Almighty that she became the magnificent witness before all the nations of God's desire to communicate with man. Israel was already the sacrament of God, the embodiment in a visible people of the grace of God given to men. Israel, as the mystery of Christ partially realized, was the visible sign of God present in man. She was at the same time a warm, living presage of an even fuller presence to come. From this seed-of-God's-union-with-man grew the Christ—Christ who would be the perfect realization in a visible human form of God's alliance with his people; Christ would unite in his very person both God's invitation to love and life, and man's response of fidelity.

8

THE FULLNESS OF REVELATION

Just as God, in the history of Israel, only gradually revealed himself in wondrous actions, so Christ, as he begins his public ministry, unveils bit by bit his true identity and the extraordinary riches he came to bring to man. He uses signs, those marvellous miracles through which he allowed his divinity to be glimpsed, much as the rays flashing through the clouds betray the piercing brightness of the sun on the other side. Thus, he attracts men's attention to the incredible dynamo of divine power clothed by his human form. "Many other signs did Jesus work in the sight of his disciples," John tells us toward the end of his gospel. "These signs are written that you might believe that Jesus is the Christ, the Son of God, and that believing you might have life in his name." (Jn 20,20f)

At the outset Jesus presents himself to John the Baptist to be baptized. As soon as Jesus comes out of the water, Matthew reports, the Spirit of God descends upon him in the form of a dove, and a voice from the heavens declares: "This is my beloved Son, in whom I am well pleased." (Mt 3,17) For John the Baptist this was a sign from God that the man he had baptized was the promised Messia. (Jn 1,29–34) Nathanael certainly recognized something great in the Nazarene, for, even though he had not been visible to Jesus, the Master told him that he had been sitting under a fig tree when Philip called him. Jesus then promised him that even greater things would he witness. (Jn 1,48ff)

Jesus worked the first of his signs in Cana at the wedding feast when he changed water into wine. (Jn 2,11) This manifestation of his glory made the disciples believe in him. He performed a second sign when he cured at a distance the son of the Capharnaum official. (Jn 2,46–54) He healed the crippled, he fed many thousands of people with but a few loaves of bread, and he gave sight to a man born blind. Indeed, Jesus even brought Lazarus back to life. This last case is particularly interesting, for after he informs his disciples that Lazarus has died and that he intends to go to him, he adds "I am glad for your sake that I was not there [at the time of his illness], that you may believe." (Jn 11,15) Just before Christ calls Lazarus from the tomb, he speaks aloud to his Father: "Father I thank you that you have heard me. Yet I knew that you always hear me. But for the people who stand around did I speak, that they may believe that you have sent me." (Jn 11,41f) As Lazarus came forth from the dead, Martha, his sister, beheld the glory of God. (v.40)

Throughout St. John's gospel we notice that the evangelist continually refers to these wondrous incidents as "signs." Christ's miracles were pointers leading those who witnessed them to realize that this man possessed a superhuman power. They therefore came to believe in his mission from God, and finally in his divinity. Yet, after so many stupendous marvels, his disciples still did not fully understand. He had to explain all that he had done. To Philip's eager request: "Lord, show us the Father and it is enough for us," Jesus replies with near exasperation:

> So long a time have I been with you, and you do not know me? Philip, he who sees me sees also the Father! How can you say, "Show us the Father"? Do you not believe that I am in the Father and the Father in me? The words that I speak to you I speak not on my own authority. But the Father dwelling in me, it is He who does the works. Do you believe that I am in the Father and the Father in me? At least believe because of the works themselves. (Jn 14,8–12)

So that the disciples will not have a shadow of doubt as to who he is and what he came to accomplish, the final and greatest of all sign-miracles comes with his being raised from the dead. In his resurrection, Christ's divinity so perfectly suffuses his humanity that for anyone who, with the eyes of faith, observes him walking about Palestine, there is no opening for disbelief, so strengthened is his faith that God was really in that man. All Jesus' miracles are signs pointing to the fact that God dwells in Christ, that Christ is the sign, the sacrament of God.

As the sacrament of God, Jesus Christ (so the Church teaches us at the Council of Chalcedon) is "one person in two natures." A divine person, the Son of God, has chosen to manifest himself in a sensible, visible human form. The second person of the Blessed Trinity is personally man, and he who has this manhood is personally God, God in a human manner. The Word of God lives his divine life in humanity, as a human being. Whatever he does as man is the act of the Son of God done in a human way; his human love is the human form of the redeeming love of God. The humanity of Jesus, then, is the concrete gift of God's grace in human form. Because his actions are the actions of God, they have a divine saving power, but, because Christ is man, this divine salvific force is given to us in an earthly, tangible form. Christ's actions are sacramental, are sacraments—God's redeeming love and life in exteriorly visible signs.

"CHRIST WITH US"

That, then, is what sacraments are: *God-given signs of his grace which actually contain that relation of love which is grace, and bestow it on us.* They are not merely human show, human transactions, or human play. They are the Word of God himself (his body now taken from our sight) in the dress of human action. Just as Christ's humanity was an instrument intimately united to the person of God's Son, so the sacraments are instrumental signs still used by that person now visibly departed from us. They are the prolongations of the incarnation of the Son of God.

As human signs, the sacraments both hide and yet tell us about their inner supernatural reality. Water is a sign of the invisible washing of the soul by God, of the burial and resurrection of total manhood. A hand upon the head making a mark upon the forehead with oil is a very human action, but it clothes the invisible touch of the Holy Spirit. Bread and wine are ordinary products of human work, yet after the powerful words are spoken by the priest they are Christ's saving body and blood. The vows of marriage sound like the frequent promises of human love; yet, at the same time, they express in audible sounds the love of Christ for his Church.

And so Christ is still with us in his signs. God continues to speak his word to us, to do his word in us, through his Christ-sign.

CHAPTER TWO

"BROUGHT TO LIFE TOGETHER WITH CHRIST"

—Eph 2,5

The resurrection of Christ was not just a sign-miracle to be seen; it was and is a sacrament of life. All will agree that what happened on the first Easter was the most stupendous of the Savior's wonders. However, the real significance of the paschal mystery for the world lies, not in its startling character, but rather in the fact that it is *the* life-giving event of Christ's life, the fulfillment of the world's deepest yearnings, core and kernel of every sacrament we celebrate today.

We have just seen what the humanity of Jesus Christ means for our salvation—that it is the sacrament of God's presence for us. In this chapter, the task that lies before us is to see that Christ's resurrection— which made Christ in his *humanity* the source of divine life for us—is what actually takes hold of us in every sacrament we celebrate; that each and every sacrament makes us sharers in Christ's risen life; that through each sacrament we become Christ's resurrected body. For the resurrection was the accomplishment of our salvation in Christ.

PRODIGAL SONS

Holy Scripture portrays salvation as the return of mankind to God. Through Adam's sin we had rejected God, wandered from the intimacy of his paternal love, and sought our happiness in proud independence among things here below which we expected to dominate in opposition to him. "You shall be as gods," the serpent had told our first parents. (Gn 3,5) To their regret, they soon discovered what sort of gods they had become. They saw their nakedness and their weakness. The world and the animals which they were meant to rule turned against them and demanded their submission. So supreme was human nature that in time men began to worship the things of this earth as possessing divine power. Finally, death came to crown their self-sufficiency. In leaving the tender love of a Father for whom their hearts longed, men fell into the embrace of the horrible and progressive degradation of self-worship, the terrifying isolation of self-love which could not but end in emptiness. Men were doomed to live this life under the wrath of God, with nothing but the silence of the grave awaiting them when breath failed.

Like a man sinking more deeply into quicksand, the human race could do nothing to heal the wound, the rebellion that separated it from God. Only God could save man. Providentially, he chose to do so. With a love that shows its profundity by giving of itself in the face of rejection, God offered himself to man in a most incredible way. Yet God would not rob man of his dignity and free will. He would not do everything for man and thus treat him like a child. He would give himself personally in the incarnation—he would come to man as man. It is as man that Christ leads mankind back to intimacy with his Father. This means that man co-operates in the saving of his own humanity. The incarnation, although

13

radically changing the human fallen condition, equips humanity with that immense power capable of transforming its corruption, rising above sin and death, and finally attaining the divine glory itself.

"IN THE FORM OF A SLAVE"

God sent his Son "in the likeness of sinful flesh." (Rom 8,3) Christ, though he was by nature divine, did not cling to his divine dignity "but emptied himself, taking the nature of a slave and being made like unto men." (Phil 2,7) Without being personally guilty of sin, he took on himself our sinful condition and the penalty to which it was subject. He was entirely free from sin himself because he was the incarnate Son of God. Nonetheless, he willingly accepted solidarity with human nature infected by sin. The Son of God took upon himself a human nature in its carnal state, that is, according to St. Paul, a state of opposition to God. His purpose, of course, was to bring man out of this condition of subservience to the flesh and subject him to the power of the spirit, a state of loving obedience to the Father. But this did not happen in a moment. It was a long and arduous movement that Christ went through. It meant a long period of debasement in which his divinity was hidden, and tied, and in which his humanity suffered the terrible consequences of sin.

VICTOR OVER DEATH

Christ's earthly life was spent in sharing our human weakness. It was a life dedicated to struggle against Satan and sin, a life that reached its climax in the final combat with death. He succumbed in the body, and yet this moment of deepest degradation was also the moment of his glory, for the loving obedience with which he accepted his passion and crucifixion brought victory out of defeat. The complete surrender that he made of himself in his death constituted a supremely meritorious sacrifice. He gave himself to his Father; he surrendered his humanity wholly and entirely to its creator. Thus he passed through the barrier which separated man from God. His humanity was now totally subject to God.

This sacrificial love of Christ merited the destruction of man's condition of sin and subjugation to evil. The resurrection was the divinizing transformation of man's humanity that brought it definitively within the sphere of the Spirit of God. God's Spirit, though present in Jesus from the beginning, was hidden. In the resurrection (taken as the type of the whole mystery of Jesus' glorification) the Spirit was released; his full effects were then felt in Christ's humanity. Our humanity in Christ was now returned to the Father; it came to enjoy the transfiguring glory of union with God. What had been formerly concealed was now fully revealed. When St. Thomas saw Christ after the resurrection, he immediately exclaimed: "My Lord and my God!" (Jn 20,28) Before, Christ had been born son of David according to the flesh, but by the resurrection he "was constituted Son of God in the glory of power, according to the spirit of holiness." (Rom 1,4)

St. Paul did not hesitate to describe Christ's rising as a second birth, quoting Ps 2,7: "You are my son; this day have I begotten you." (Ac 13,33) The resurrection gave birth in the humanity of Christ to the life of the Son of God, extended to it the glory of the eternally generated Word. The same Christ who, not clinging to his divinity, had emptied himself, taking upon himself the form of a slave, humbled himself even to the death of the cross. In response, "God exalted and bestowed upon him the name that is above every name, so that at the name of Jesus every knee should bend of those in heaven, on earth and under the earth, and that every tongue should confess that the Lord Jesus Christ is in the glory of God the Father." (Phil 2,9ff) A name that provokes the adoration of all creatures can indicate nothing else but the majesty of God and his dominion over all things. Christ himself after his resurrection did indeed proclaim: "All power in heaven and on earth has been given to me." (Mt 28,18)

TWO ASPECTS
OF A UNIQUE MYSTERY

Christ's death and resurrection are equally essential to the redemptive plan. As St. Paul writes, "Christ was delivered up for our sins and rose again for our justification." (Rom 4,25) A rebellious human race had to be brought back to God. For this, two things were required: surrender of the rebel and God's acceptance of his obedient return. It is clear that the most important function was played by God's acceptance, for without it no amount of self-surrender would save. A son may protest over and over again his sorrow for having offended his father, but until the father speaks his forgiveness there is no reconciliation. Salvation can come only from God. At the same time God will not force his divine life upon anyone. Man must turn toward him, open his heart to his grace, be converted.

In this way, both Christ's passion and resurrection concur in achieving our redemption. The first is the surrender of sinful mankind to God; the second is God's specifically divine transforming action by which he pours his divine life into human nature, once weak and sin-laden, now radically changed into having a share in the divine nature. Christ's death was man asking forgiveness through God's only Son; his resurrection was God granting forgiveness and receiving prodigal humanity back into the intimacy of a father's love—yet even more, adopting man as his son on a higher level than before.

This is why St. Paul warns the Corinthians: "If Christ has not risen, vain is your faith, for you are still in your sins." (1 Cor 15,17) In other words, if Christ has not risen, there is no redemption. Although Christ's self-surrender was absolutely necessary for salvation, it was nonetheless the human prerequisite. The act that redeemed us is the action of God transforming the humanity of Christ, delivering him from this world of sin and death, suffusing him with the Spirit and glorifying him, making him the source of life for those who believe in him.

Christ's death, accepted by him as it was with sacrificial love, truly merited salvation. His death as a mere biological fact was not redemptive in the least. But if any sincere request for forgiveness, any heartfelt gift of self, merits some consideration on the part of the person to whom it is offered, all the more so his request and his gift. For what made his death meritorious was the fact that it proceeded from the loving obedience of his will with which he freely cooperated as God-man with the divine will. This was the greatest act of love possible for man. It was the lowest point of Christ's debasement, yet because he was obedient it was the climactic expression of his love. "Greater love than this no man has than that a man lay down his life for his friends." (Jn 15,13) Such self-surrender, such death, was already in point of fact life-giving, for the total, loving obedience motivating it merited God's vivifying salvific act, the resurrection, both for Christ and all his brethren.

The Lord's death and resurrection are essential to redemption, we

16

have said, as two aspects of a unique mystery. The remission of sin and the infusion of divine life are intrinsically and indispensably connected with each other as two necessary parts of the same act of reconciliation. One cannot be had without the other, as St. Paul's summation in Romans 4,25 suggests: "Christ was delivered up for our sins and rose again for our justification." The first was a turning away from sin and a self-surrender to God; the second was God's acceptance of his prodigal child, the reopening of his paternal heart to his offspring, the restitution to the wanderer of the full, intimate life of his Father.

It is in this central mystery of Christ's life that we find the full blossoming of the sacramental expression of God's saving act of love. Because Christ is the efficacious sign of God's redemptive design, his every action is an expression of the divine love and power. Christ's whole life, then, effectively manifested and brought to men his Father's saving love. But this process achieved its completion and eternal permanence in the risen Christ seated in glory at the right hand of his Father. *The very essence of this redemptive drama, therefore, was Christ's death and resurrection, for in this twofold action occurred the definitive transition of Christ's human nature from its fallen state to the state of new life in God.* This is why we call the paschal mystery the sacrament of the divine redemptive act, the efficacious sign of God transforming man into his adoptive son. In other words, what was brought about in Christ is the sacrament of the same transfiguration to be effected in all men. The act that glorified Christ glorifies us. Christ's role as the sacrament of the Father's love for men is epitomized, summed up, in the mystery of his death and resurrection.

"IN CHRIST JESUS"

So permeated was the Savior's humanity with the Spirit of God that it became "life-giving spirit" (1 Cor 15,45), the dynamic principle of divine life in us. Whereas his earthly life had been spent in sharing our fallen humanity, through his resurrection he was made Son of God *for us,* capable of sharing with us his divine sonship. This is the whole point of St. Paul's description of that event as a second birth of the Son of God. (Rom 1,4; Ac 13,33) The same sinful flesh which the Word had taken *17*
from David's line was now regenerated as divine.

Our human nature arose resplendent with God's own life! Even when we were dead by reason of our sin, St. Paul insists, God "brought us to life together with Christ, and raised us up together, and seated us together in heaven in Christ Jesus." (Eph 2,5f) This was God's *plan* from eternity, the *mystery* of his love.

> Blessed be the God and Father of our Lord Jesus Christ, who has blessed us with every spiritual blessing on high in Christ. Even as he chose us in him before the foundation of the world, that we should be holy and without blemish before him in love. He pre-destined us to be adopted through Jesus Christ as his sons, according to the purpose of his will. (Eph 1,3ff)

Poignantly does St. Paul bring this out in his use of the notion of "first-fruits." "Christ has risen from the dead, the first-fruits of those who have fallen asleep. . . . As in Adam all die, so in Christ all will be made to live. But each in his own turn, Christ as first-fruits, then they who are Christ's, who have believed at his coming." (1 Cor 15,20–23) That this idea applied not only to the final resurrection is clear from a similar ex-pression in Colossians 1, 18ff. Just as God's Son is the firstborn of every creature, because in him all things were created, so "he is the head of his body, the Church; he who is the beginning, the firstborn from the dead, that in all things he may have the first place. For it has pleased God the Father that in him all his fullness should dwell, and that through him he should reconcile to himself all things." All are contained in Christ, as in him our human nature rises from the dead.

As a result of his redemptive resurrection, he had released his Spirit for us. God sent his Son that he might redeem us, "that we might receive the adoption of sons. And because we are sons, God has sent the Spirit of his Son into our hearts, crying 'Abba, Father.'" (Gal 4,5f) Be-cause Christ put to death our carnal humanity and gave us a glorified human nature, a nature imbued with his Spirit, we have a right to glory in our divine sonship, newly won through Jesus Christ, "through whom we also have access by faith unto that grace in which we stand, and exult in the hope of the glory of the sons of God" (Rom 5,2)—so long, of course, as we live according to his Spirit and not according to the flesh. (8,5–13)

18   We can glory in divine sonship only insofar as we personally follow Christ in this movement back to the Father. Just as Christ was not an

inanimate tool in the hands of God but cooperated with a free act of love, so we are not saved by having to be driven into the divine life. Like Christ, we are required to sacrifice the ways of fallen flesh and enter with love into the realm of his spirit.

At the same time, this is not accomplished by a mere act of our free will. We must become part of Christ's risen body, for his humanity is the only channel of salvation. To be sons of God we must become other Christs; we have to be taken up in the very act of the Savior's resurrection and participate in the resurrection body of the Lord. Again Paul pointedly remarks: "Therefore, my brethren, you also, through the body of Christ, have been made to die to the Law, so as to belong to another, to him who has risen from the dead, in order to bring forth fruit unto God." (Rom 7,4) Throughout his epistles, we find Paul using very strong language to show that we can obtain the new life—return to the Father—only by being joined to the risen Christ. He insists on the real identification of Christians with the body of Christ.

> As the body is one and has many members, and all the members of the body, many as they are, form one body, so also is it with Christ. For in one Spirit we were all baptized into one body, whether Jews or gentiles, whether slaves or free. . . . Now you are the body of Christ, member for member. (1 Cor 12,12f.27)*

"For all you who have been baptized into Christ, have put on Christ. . . . You are all one in Christ. And if you are Christ's, then you are the offspring of Abraham, heirs according to promise." (Gal 3,27ff) The last part of this quotation is particularly interesting, for it really means that even the gentiles, when they come to believe in Christ, enter the race of Abraham. This can be true only if the Christian is united to the bodily humanity of the Lord. Adhesion to Christ makes us descendants of Abraham only if it unites us to the Savior's body, for his body is the only bond between him and his forefathers. Or again,

> He himself is our peace, who has made both [peoples: Jew and gentile] one, breaking down the wall of partition between them, enmity, having made void in his flesh the Law of the commandments with its prescriptions so that both [peoples] may form one new man in him, so that he may reconcile both to God in a single body. (Eph 2,14ff)

---

* A period between verse numbers indicates that the verses cited are successive but nonconsecutive.

This identification between the Christian and Christ in the one life of his risen and glorified body is brought out constantly in Paul's use of the expression "in Christ." "You are in Christ Jesus, who has become for us God-given wisdom, and justice, and sanctification and redemption." (1 Cor 1,30) "There is now therefore no condemnation for those who are in Christ Jesus, who do not walk according to the flesh. For the life-giving law of the Spirit in Christ Jesus has delivered me from the law of sin and of death." (Rom 8,1f) "If any man is in Christ, he is a new creature." (2 Cor 5,17) "The gift of God is life everlasting in Christ Jesus our Lord." (Rom 6,23)

To emphasize the same message, St. Paul often employs a formula which is the reverse of the above: "Know you not that Christ Jesus is in you?" (2 Cor 13,5) He considered himself in labor "until Christ be formed" in his disciples. (Gal 4,19) He could even say that "it is no longer I that live, but Christ lives in me." (Gal 2,20) What all this means is that in his death and resurrection Christ was changed from a living soul into a life-giving spirit. His body, freed from carnal enslavement to the devil and sin, became spirit—became divinized. Hence, Christ in his bodily humanity became capable of giving life to men. The very life of his transfigured human nature he communicates to us, bringing us into the new life of his risen body, clothing us in his new being, making us over into himself.

To say that we should "become the body of Christ" is to use language that is almost shocking. We must admit that the Hebrew concept of the body was not exactly the same as ours. Paul, like a good Semite, did not divide human nature, as we do, into distinct and separable parts: the material body and the soul or life-principle in it. His was a more comprehensive conception of human nature. As we saw above, he consistently uses a personal pronoun for the body, because for him it means the whole human person. The body designates the whole man because the human being is present and expresses himself in his material corporealness. To belong to the body of Christ, therefore, means to belong to Christ, to live in him, of him. The accent remains on the material element, however, for it was in and with his body that Christ saved us —that God raised us from the dead. We belong, therefore, to a bodily Christ.

20

We ought also to note in passing that "body" in St. Paul's writings is not really the same as "flesh." Nor is "body" opposed logically to "spirit." By "flesh" he understands fallen human nature, the body as infected by sin and inclined to evil. "Spirit," on the other hand, is the body redeemed and set under the sway of God's love and life. The body can be the bearer of either relationship.

We are, therefore, really and truly united to Christ's physical body of the resurrection. Paul does not simply say that the Church is like the body of Christ. He says she *is* the body of Christ. The Church is indeed the body of Christ because she is united in each and all her members to the risen body of the Lord.

This doctrine of St. Paul has been taken up by the Church's oldest and most venerated teachers, the Fathers and Doctors. St. John Chrysostom writes that Christ "unites himself to us and makes us his body, not only in faith, but in reality. . . . We are nourished by him, we unite ourselves to him, we become one body of Christ, one flesh." (*Commentaries on Matthew, John, and I Corinthians; PG* 58,743; 59,260–62; 61,199–201) St. Augustine also insists that we are made the body of him, and by the mercy of him whom we receive, we exist. No less explicit is St. John Damascene: "Because we partake of a single bread, we all become a single body of Christ, a single blood, and members one of another, being made of one body with Christ." (*On Orthodox Faith,* 4,13; *PG* 94,1153) To quote one more witness from somewhat later times, St. Albert the Great writes: "One can see no reason why the Church should be called the body of Christ, and should in fact be so, except because, by giving her his body, Christ transforms her into himself so that she may become his body and all may become his members." (*On the Eucharist,* 3,1,v.5)

THE PASCHAL MYSTERY
IN THE SACRAMENTS

There is no question here, of course, of participating in the life of Christ's body which he had in the carnal phase of his humanity when he was still under the sentence of sin. Hardly, for we already have that kind of life by birth. The startling event of two thousand years ago is precisely that God saves us and divinizes us by causing us to be reborn in that body of his Son in which sin was destroyed, and in which and from which the holiness and life of his Spirit springs forth. The risen body of Christ is indeed the Church's native soil, the very root of her existence.

The principle of all Christian existence, then, is a constant participation in Christ's death and resurrection. Life is a dynamic thing, Christ's life no less than anyone else's. To live in Christ demands a real sharing in the very act by which Christ in his humanity was reborn Son of God.

The sacraments are the means for achieving our immersion in Christ's redemptive act. Just as Christ was the sacrament of the Father's love and life, just as the passion and resurrection concretized his sacramental role in the redemption of mankind, so this saving mystery passes to us in the sacraments of the Church. In them we are assimilated into Christ's resurrected body.

If St. Paul is so explicit about the reality of our union with the risen body of Christ, he is no less forceful when he comes to speak of the way we genuinely participate in Christ's very own act of dying and rising again. "You were buried together with Christ in *baptism,* and in him also rose again." (Col 2,12) He pursues this theme more at length in Romans 6:

> Do you not know that all we who have been baptized into Christ Jesus have been baptized into his death? For we were buried with him by means of baptism into death, in order that, just as Christ has arisen from the dead through the glory of the Father, so we also may walk in newness of life. For if we have been united with him in the likeness of his death, we shall be so in the likeness of his resurrection also. . . . If we have died with Christ, we believe that we shall also live together with Christ. (vv.3ff.8)

Though this text affirms explicitly only our sharing in Christ's resurrection some time in the future, it is clear that Paul understands it as a permanent contact which subjects our entire life to God's action in raising up Christ. For he concludes in the same chapter: "Thus do you consider yourselves also as dead to sin but alive to God in Christ Jesus . . . Do not let sin reign in your mortal body . . . but present yourselves to God as those who have come to life from the dead and your members as weapons of justice for God." (vv.11–13)

And again: "With Christ I am nailed to the cross. It is no longer I that live, but Christ lives in me." (Gal 2,19f) As the years bring him closer to bodily death, he is nonetheless strong in the life of Christ: "Even

22

though our outer man is decaying, yet our inner man is being renewed day by day." (2 Cor 4,16) He gladly accepts all his sufferings that he may gain Christ and be found in him and thus know "the power of his resurrection and the fellowship of his sufferings." (Phil 3, 8ff)

The whole life of the Christian, then, is under the power of Christ's resurrection because of the sacraments he receives; he continually receives the vivifying action of Christ because he joins himself to his Savior's body that is risen from the dead. Paul insists that both Christ and the faithful are subject to one and the same life-giving action of God: "He brought us to life *together* with Christ and raised us up together." (Eph 2,5f) This is what he means, then, when he says that we "are baptized into the death of Christ." (Rom 6,3)

The same must be said of the *eucharist* in which we feast on the very body and blood of the resurrected Christ. St. Paul reminds the Corinthians that "as often as you eat this bread and drink this cup you proclaim the death of the Lord until he comes." (1 Cor 10,26) He certainly did not mean that the eucharist brings death to us, but rather that our eating of the eucharist is our most intimate means of sharing in Christ's victory over the death of sin, of immersing ourselves in Christ's passing over from the evil of Satan's domination to new life under God's love. The Savior himself is reported by St. John to have said: "If anyone eat of this bread he shall live forever; and the bread that I will give is my flesh for the life of the world." (Jn 6,52)

It is not the dead Christ whom we eat in the eucharistic celebration; it is the Christ who died once for all to sin and who now lives unto God. (Rom 6,10) The basic symbolism of the sacrament is precisely one of life, for it is a sacred meal in which God gives himself and his life to us in the form of food. Through this incredible sacrament we touch directly and primarily the Lord's resurrection, and through it make contact with his death. The eucharist is the most perfect of all the sacraments for it brings Christ's redemptive act to us in all its original freshness, uniqueness and vitality—so much so that, in eating of Christ's risen body, we must show the difference in ourselves. We must "proclaim the death of the Lord" (1 Cor 10,26), show that we have died to sin and have arisen with Christ to the Father.

Confirmation also makes us sharers in Christ's death and resurrection. Recall that wonderful episode in Acts (8,15ff) wherein Peter and John arrive in Samaria and call down the Holy Spirit upon those who

23

had already been baptized in the name of Jesus. The giving of the Spirit of God is the first result of the death and resurrection of Christ, as we have already seen.

The same is true of the sacrament of *penance*, for on the evening of the resurrection the Lord appears to his disciples, breathes upon them, and says; "Receive the Holy Spirit; whose sins you shall forgive they are forgiven, and whose sins you shall retain they are retained." (Jn 20,22) Reconciliation in the Spirit was the whole purpose of Christ's death and resurrection.

Concerning the sacrament of *ordination* Paul urges Timothy to "stir up the grace of God which is in you through the laying on of my hands." (1 Tim 1,6) A man is configured to Christ the redeemer through the laying on of hands, for what is grace but that tremendous reality which God puts in us to make us over into the likeness of his Son. The immediate source of that grace can only be the death and resurrection of Christ.

Christian *marriage* also steeps us more deeply in the paschal mystery, for St. Paul calls it "a great mystery, I mean in relation to Christ and to the Church." (Eph 5,32) He is not referring to a symbolic relationship of marriage to Christ's union with the Church. All marriage, whether Christian or not, already mirrors such devotion. Rather he is saying that Christian marriage is an imitation of that divine-human union and proceeds from it, represents it by showing it operative and grace-giving in itself. Christ became head of the Church through his death and resurrection: "Christ delivered himself up for her that he might sanctify her. . . ." (vv.25f) Christian marriage continues efficaciously the love of Christ for his Church and shares in its sanctifying effect.

Finally the *anointing of the sick* extends the saving power of the paschal mystery to us in the final combat for our souls' salvation, as we strive to die in union with Christ on the cross to prepare for our glorious entry into heaven. St. James advises us in his epistle: "Is any one among you sick? Let him bring in the presbyters of the church, and let them pray over him, anointing him with oil in the name of the Lord. And the prayer of faith will save the sick man, and the Lord will raise him up, and if he be in sins, they shall be forgiven him." (Jas 5,14f) According to St. James this sacred rite may even infuse the infirmed body of man with the saving power of the resurrection, should such be God's will. Whether restoration of bodily health or final preparation of the soul for

24

entry into heaven be the result, the effect is accomplished by the "anointing in the name of the Lord," Jesus who saves through his death and resurrection.

"FROM GLORY TO GLORY"

Each sacrament does its bit, according to the various phases of our human life and our role in the Church, to deepen our incorporation into the risen Christ and thus push forward our movement of return to our heavenly Father. In doing this each sacrament continues Christ, the sacrament par excellence of the Father's loving, vivifying, and transfiguring presence. By allowing ourselves to be inserted into Christ's risen body through the sacraments, we communicate in Christ's own resurrection and receive in him God's glorifying action.

Signs effectively bringing us the glorious God-man, the sacraments resurrect us bit by bit and transform us into the image and likeness of Christ, the glory of the Father. "We all, with faces unveiled, reflecting as in a mirror the glory of the Lord, are being transformed into his very image from glory to glory, as through the Spirit of the Lord." (2 Cor 3,18) Thus, as other Christs, are we prepared for fullest participation in the love of the Father. Yes, our bodies too, for they are Christ.

But as each sacrament brings us further into the resurrection of Christ, we are also reminded that the crucifixion was the road to it. To be fully other Christs in glory we have to surrender ourselves with his sacrificial love. St. Paul warns us realistically:

> Therefore, if you have risen with Christ, seek the things that are above, where Christ is seated at the right hand of God. Mind the things that are above, not the things that are of earth [meaning an earth opposed to God]. For you have died and your life is hidden with Christ in God. When Christ, your life, shall appear, then you too will appear with him, all glorious. (Col 3,1–4)

CHAPTER THREE

"MEDIATOR OF A NEW COVENANT"

—Heb 9,15

Far from being obstacles that draw our attention to themselves and prevent our approach to Christ, the sacraments lead us to Christ, insert us into his glorified humanity, transform us into himself. Nor do they operate independently of him, for sacraments are actions of Christ the redeemer.

Sacraments have no meaning except as actions of Christ; from him they receive their efficacy and content. They are simply visible signs containing the original redeeming act of Christ. However, this does not imply that that act is repeated for us. Christ died once for all, Paul tells us (Rom 6,10); the Savior entered once for all through the greater and more perfect tabernacle. (Heb 9,11.26ff; 10,12ff) Consequently, there can be no question of a repetition of his sacrifice. On the other hand, neither are we led back into the past to that single moment of the redemption; for man lives in time—he cannot reverse it. Indeed, he does not have to, for redemption is always available in the glorified Christ who, though bodily gone from our eyes, is ever present to men of all ages.

ETERNAL REDEEMER

Yet, as we have seen, St. Paul's teaching describes a sharing, not only in Christ's glorified state, but in the very act of his being glorified. The Savior's passing over from the death of sin to the new life under God must retain a permanent actuality, and it does. The Father's life-giving action on Christ's humanity belongs to God's eternity. Christ at his rising becomes immovably and unchangeably glorified, but, as we saw, his very dying achieves its goal—his glorification. Hence, at this moment Christ in his humanity reaches eternity, the bosom of the Father, and is thus beatified. He is eternally fixed in the very act of redeeming us. He is caught and held fast forever at the very summit of his redemptive activity. The never-to-be-repeated sacrifice is eternally actual in the very fullness of its goal, Christ's resurrection. The death and resurrection which took place so long ago continue to happen then—not to Christ, but to us each time we are incorporated more fully into him through the sacraments.

Christ, dynamically held in the act of rising from the dead, is the one who makes each sacrament productive within us of that same death to sin and resurrection to the life of his Father. The Lord simply sacramentalizes his permanent act of salvation for us, turns his everlasting intercession before the throne of his Father into visible form for us to grasp. This is the most basic meaning of the Church's dogma that Christ instituted the sacraments. They owe their very existence and effectiveness right here and now to Jesus Christ. Regardless of the ordinary appearance 27 of the sacramental signs, regardless of the minister's condition of soul, power passes through the sacraments, and that power comes directly from the sacred glorified humanity of Christ in the act of redeeming us.

"A PRIEST FOREVER"

In his epistles, St. Paul insists over and over again that through his resurrection Christ became life-giving for us. This was his entry into his universal lordship, and his domination is exercised first and foremost in redemptive activity. Throughout his life, according to Hebrews, but especially in his transfiguring sacrifice, Christ was and is a priest, a mediator between God and men.

> Christ did not glorify himself with the high priesthood, but he [did] who said to him, "You are my son, I have this day begotten you." As he says also in another place, "You are a priest forever according to the order of Melchisedech." For Jesus, in the days of his earthly life, with a loud cry and tears, offered up prayers and supplications to him who was able to save him from death, and was heard because of his reverent submission. And Son though he was, he learned obedience from the things that he suffered; and when perfected, he became to all who obey him the cause of eternal salvation, called by God a high priest according to the order of Melchisedech. (Heb 5,5–10)

Though Christ had a priesthood from the first moment of his incarnation, being both God and man, there was a certain "perfection" lacking to it. That perfection came with what we might call the public proclamation of his Father's decree making him a priest. At the moment of Christ's sacrifice, the "hour" of his supreme exaltation, the Father accepted the Son's humanity, made and proclaimed it the dispenser of his divine life to men.

A priest is one who "is taken from among men and appointed for men in the things pertaining to God, that he may offer gifts and sacrifices for sins." (Heb 5,1) The appointment, as we have seen, must be made by God. And that appointment, or consecration, in the case of Christ's humanity, came at his resurrection, for this was the occasion of God's oath: "You are a priest forever. . . ." Other texts in Hebrews continue this theme. "We have a high priest who has passed into the heavens, Jesus the Son of God." (4,14) "It was fitting that we should have such a high priest, holy, innocent, undefiled, set apart from sinners, and become higher than the heavens." (7,26) "We have such a high priest,

28

who has taken his seat at the right hand of the throne of Majesty in the heavens, a minister of the Holies and of the true tabernacle which the Lord has erected and not man." (8,1f) "If then he were on earth, he would not even be a priest, since there are already others to offer gifts according to the Law." (8,4)

In the Mosaic Law, promulgated under God's authority, a priest had to be born of the tribe of Levi. Christ did not take his humanity from that tribe. If he were to be a priest, God would have to by-pass the Law which he himself had established. This he did, for Christ in his incarnation was the most perfect of priests, combining in his own person both God and man. But that humanity was still under the yoke of the Law and under the burden of man's sin. It was his sacrificial glorification —his death, resurrection, and ascension—which proclaimed his priesthood. According to the words of Hebrews, Christ's entry into glory is his priestly consecration. The entire activity of the risen Christ is a priestly dispensing of divine life to men.

The figure of Melchisedech is also important here. This priest of ancient times was "without father, without mother, without genealogy, having neither beginning of days nor end of life, but likened to the Son of God, he continues a priest forever." (Heb 7,3) Scripture portrays Melchisedech as someone who had no human generation, who had no end—as one, therefore, having a lasting priesthood. When the Father proclaims his Son "a priest forever, according to the order of Melchisedech," he is saying that his Son has an endless priesthood. It is the equivalent when we are told that Christ, "when perfected, became the cause of *eternal* salvation." (5,9) Because our high priest has reached immortality and dwells in heaven, there is no limit to his role of imparting to men the salvation he won for them. Later, Hebrews says quite explicitly: "Because he continues forever, he has an everlasting priesthood. Therefore he is able at all times to save those who come to God through him, since he lives always to make intercession for them." (7, 24f)

"A LAMB
STANDING AS IF SLAIN"

To be a priest means to be the channel of exchange between God and man, an offerer of sacrifice. If Christ is our high priest in heaven,

29

what kind of sacrifice can he possibly be offering? During his vision, reported in the Apocalypse, St. John beholds in the midst of the heavenly court "a lamb standing as if slain." (5,6) He is standing, a posture which symbolizes life. At the same time he has the appearance of having been killed. In other words, in heaven the Savior bears in his person the sign of his sacrifice. St. John also brings this out in his gospel where much is made of the Savior's wounds when Christ lets Thomas examine them. (Jn 20,24–27) A strange thing indeed: unhealed wounds in a glorified body! The insistence of Hebrews that every high priest must have "something to offer" and that Christ is our high priest in heaven (Heb 8,1–5) shows that the presence of such wounds in eternity is not merely a reminder of the Lord's passion. These wounds are the means of an ever actual and permanent sacrifice. Christ is truly "a minister of the Holies."

The epistle constantly alludes to the value and power of the blood of Christ. The Savior entered into the Holies not by virtue of the blood of goats and calves, as in the Old Testament, "but by virtue of his own blood, having obtained eternal redemption." (9,12) If the blood of the animal victims of old was useful for sanctification under the Old Law, "how much more will the blood of Christ, who through the Holy Spirit offered himself unblemished unto God, cleanse your conscience." (v.14) Our consciences are cleansed by an ever-present victim. We find entry into the Holies "in the blood of Christ, a new and living way which he has begun for us through the veil, that is, his flesh." (10,19f) Christ's blood is our way to heaven; he has paved the way there by the *opening* in his own flesh. The author likens the Lord's flesh to the veil of the Holy of Holies; this vein which barred our approach to God is now open to us. His blood, his torn flesh, are now instruments of reconciliation with the Father; they are the Savior's means of continuing to plead our cause before the Father. His blood "speaks better than Abel," Hebrews says (12,24), using the present tense.

If Christ is our priest in heaven, he must have a sacrifice. This is himself, his body and blood, a victim for us. Yet recall that Paul rejects any possibility of a repetition, a redoing of that sacrifice. Christ gave himself once for all to the Father, and in that instant was glorified by his Father's accepting him. We must conclude that Paul's teaching means that Christ's sacrifice in some way perdures in heaven.

This brings us back to the solution we have already given. We are

30

involved in the difference between time and eternity. Christ died in time, true, but at that very moment, at the climax of his sacrificial human life, he reached the goal of sacrifice, glorification of his human nature. The sacrificial offering took place in the past, in time, but its acceptance by the Father—the glory it achieved—this is everlastingly actual. Christ our victim is unvaryingly, unchangeably, forever, a glorified victim. His sacrifice becomes eternally fixed at its climactic point, its goal, its final fulfillment—God's acceptance of his humanity in an embrace of love. What point was that? Christ's resurrection.

EARTHLY FORM
OF A HEAVENLY REALITY

The glorified Christ of eternity does not change; he is forever at the climactic moment of his sacrifice, but we are in time; we do change as we go from moment to moment. He, the "cause of eternal salvation," becomes present to us in sacraments. In acting on us through the sacraments, Christ is merely temporalizing what is forever actual in heaven: the Savior begging his Father to receive prodigal man back into his paternal love, and the Father giving that love. All this is one action in heaven—one glorious act of unspeakable union between the Father and our humanity in Christ. He is now in eternity at that same "moment" of saving us, but he is no longer dead; rather he is in the perfection or consecration of his death—his passing from earthly life to the divine life of the Word. In him our humanity, while remaining human, is glorified by union with his Father. This is what he does to us in time by means of the sacramental signs.

In the sacraments we encounter not a mere human priest, not simply bread and wine, water or chrism. These are but earthly veils that disguise, even while they disclose, a really and truly present Christ dying to human weakness and mortality and rising to the glorifying union with his Father *in us*. How right St. Leo was when he said: "What was visible in Christ our redeemer has passed into the sacraments of the Church!" (*Sermon 74; PL 54,398*)

CHAPTER FOUR

"BY HIS SPIRIT WHO DWELLS IN YOU"

—Rom 8,11

The whole Christian experience is under the active direction of the Holy Spirit. Always to be in contact with the Spirit, to be a living witness to the continual outpouring of the Spirit of Jesus crucified and risen, is the extreme good fortune of the Christian. Though the Holy Spirit is invisible, to those who see with faith he is very much manifest in the Christlikeness of the Church's members. As Pius XII teaches: "It is he who through his heavenly grace is the principle of every supernatural act in all parts of the [Mystical] Body. It is he who, while personally present and divinely active in all the members, also acts in the inferior members through the ministry of the higher members." (*Mystici Corporis,* America Press edition, 69)

Since he is the source of every vital salutary act of the Christian, the Spirit is also the power within the sacramental actions of Christ. Nothing in the Christian life escapes his all-pervading influence. Whereas Christ is the redeemer of mankind, the Holy Spirit is our sanctifier. In the Nicene Creed we confess him to be the "life-giving Lord": *"Dominum vivificantem."* In another of her professions of faith the Church speaks more explicitly of "the inestimable and invisible power of the Holy Spirit operative in the sacraments." (D 424[793])

The Holy Spirit is indeed at work in the sacraments. The sacramental signs are marvelously fruitful in developing within us the life of Christ precisely because of the Spirit's all-enveloping activity. How well did Simon Magus recognize the tremendous power of the sacraments. In Acts 8,18f we read that when he saw that the Holy Spirit was given through the laying on of the apostles' hands, he offered them money, entreating: "Give me also this power, so that anyone on whom I lay my hands may receive the Holy Spirit." The apostles refused, of course, but Simon's request, evil though it was, testified to the wondrous power behind the sacraments already clearly recognized in the apostolic age.

THE SPIRIT OF JESUS

This emphasis on the Spirit's activity in the sacraments seemingly contradicts the central message of the last chapter. There we said that it is Christ who acts in the sacraments to make us over into his resurrected body. Now we add that the sacraments receive their power from the Holy Spirit. True, sanctification means becoming Christ, entering into his dying and rising, into his own act of redemption. At the same time, incorporation into the risen Christ is brought about by the Spirit. Christ's original saving action is indeed in the sacraments; however, the Holy Spirit brings that saving act of Christ to us and makes it bear fruit within us. For, if one thing stands out clearly in the text of the New

33

Testament it is this: Christ's dying and rising released the Holy Spirit upon mankind. He is sent by the Father and Christ. His mission is precisely to bring forth divine life in us, to make us God's adoptive sons, to form Christ in us. He is indeed the "Spirit of Jesus." (Jn 7,37ff; Ac 16,7; Rom 8,9.11; 2 Cor 3,17; Gal 4,6; Phil 1,19)

The Holy Spirit is none other than the paschal Spirit; for on Pentecost day when Peter addressed all the visitors in Jerusalem from various parts of the Mediterranean basin—pilgrims who were awe-struck at the extraordinary fact that they heard the apostles speaking in their own tongues—he explained that his companions were not drunk but rather filled with the Spirit of Jesus whom the Jews had crucified: "This Jesus God has raised up, and we are witnesses to it. Therefore, exalted by the right hand of God, and receiving from the Father the promise of the Holy Spirit, he has poured forth this Spirit whom you see and hear." (Ac 2, 32f) The Master had warned his disciples not to leave Jerusalem but to wait for the "promise of the Father of which you have heard from my mouth. . . . You shall be baptized with the Holy Spirit not many days hence." (1,4f) Luke reports the same promise in his gospel: "I send forth upon you the promise of my Father. But wait here in the city until you are clothed with power from on high." (Lk 24,49)

While it is clear to Luke that the coming of the Spirit was the direct result of the Lord's glorification, his resurrection and ascension, John makes the connection with the resurrection more obvious. On the very eve of his death Jesus tells his apostles that he must die in order to bring them the Holy Spirit. "It is expedient for you that I depart. For if I do not go, the Advocate will not come to you; but if I go, I will send him to you." (Jn 16,7) And then on the evening of his resurrection the Savior appears to the disciples and breathing upon them says: "Receive the Holy Spirit." (Jn 20,22) We see, then, that for St. John the coming of the Spirit was not delayed until the Lord's ascension. His return to the Father was already accomplished in his death and resurrection. The ascension was but the visible manifestation of the return of Christ's humanity to the Father—essentially brought about in the glorious trans-formation of his resurrection.

In what he has to say of two other episodes of our Lord's life, St. John stresses even more explicitly the fact that the outpouring of the Holy Spirit is an Easter event. The first was an agricultural feast, that of Tabernacles, which had strong messianic overtones. On the last and

34

great day of the week-long feast a priest carried water from the Pool of Siloam in a golden jug to the Temple by way of the Water Gate amid the sound of trumpets, shouts of *hosanna* and waving of palms. It was then that the Savior cried out above the din: "If any man thirst, let him come to me; let him that believes in me drink. As the Scripture says, 'Out of his [Messia's] belly shall flow rivers of living water.'" (Jn 7,37f) St. John then explains: "He said this of the Spirit whom they who believed in him were to receive; for the Spirit had not yet been given, since Jesus had not yet been glorified." (v.39) Christ's risen humanity is the source of the Holy Spirit.

By our Lord's time water had become symbolic of the Spirit. Just as water brought life to the parched earth, so the Spirit was the source of divine life for men. "You shall draw waters with joy out of the fountains of salvation." (Is 12,3; cf. also Is 58,11; Ez 47,1–12) "I will pour out waters upon the thirsty ground. . . . I will pour out my spirit upon your seed." (Is 44,3) The waters that sprang up and saved the people in the desert will appear once again in that new rock, the Messia. (Is 48,21; 49,10; Ez 36,25f) The groundwork for this episode had already been laid by Christ during his conversation with the Samaritan woman at Jacob's well when he spoke of "living water" (Jn 4,10): "Everyone who drinks of this water [from Jacob's well] will thirst again. He, however, who drinks of the water that I will give him shall never thirst; but the water that I will give him shall become in him a fountain of water, springing up unto life everlasting." (vv.13f)

The second occasion on which St. John associates the coming of the Spirit with the paschal mystery is at the crucifixion itself. After having perceived the full prophetic import of "living water," John witnesses the actual fulfillment of the messianic promise. When the soldiers came to Jesus, "and saw that he was already dead, they did not break his legs; but one of the soldiers opened his side with a lance, and immediately there came out *blood* and *water*." (Jn 19,34) So significant was this that John feels the need of stressing his own truthfulness in reporting the event: "And he who saw this has borne witness, and his witness is true." (v.35) Almost unanimously the Fathers of the Church follow him in seeing symbolized in the water flowing from Christ's pierced side the life-giving Spirit: Irenaeus, Origen, Cyprian, Jerome, Rufinus, Ambrose, Hippolytus—to mention but a few. Invariably they hark back to the rock struck by Moses in the desert to quench his people's thirst. (Ex 17,6)

Christ was for them the rock which, once struck open by the passion, let flow the rivers of the Spirit.

CHRIST RAISED BY THE SPIRIT

But why was the gift of the Spirit dependent upon Christ's glorification? The humanity of Christ became the source of the Spirit for other men only through being itself divinized by the Spirit. St. Paul, as we have seen, was particularly aware of the genuinely fallen condition of the human nature Christ had assumed. Though he was not sinful himself, the Lord nonetheless had to redeem our sinful humanity in his own flesh. This required his complete self-surrender to the Father by means of his death on the cross. Humanity's affection for sin thus broken, it became in Christ a fitting receptacle for the Spirit of God. St. Paul pointedly remarks: "If the Spirit of him who raised up Jesus from the dead dwell in you, he who raised up Jesus Christ from the dead will also bring life to your mortal bodies by the power of the Spirit who dwells in you." (Rom 8,11) Though the Father is the one who stands behind the action of raising Christ, it is through the Spirit that it is accomplished. The glorification of Christ's humanity, after all, was but the result of its being flooded with grace. And throughout Scripture grace bears a very special relationship to the person of the Holy Spirit; grace is a participation in the Holy Spirit who is the love of Father and Son.

The same idea continues in St. Paul's epistles under other images. "Although he was crucified through weakness, yet he lives through the power of God." (2 Cor 13,4) Or again he tells the Ephesians that he prays for them that God may grant them the spirit of wisdom to know the exceeding greatness of "his power toward us who believe. Its measure is the working of his mighty power which he has wrought in Christ in raising him from the dead." (Eph 1,19f) The expression "power of God" has a strong Old Testament background. It became practically synonymous in the Hebrew Scriptures with the *ruah Yahweh,* God's spirit. It was his creative power in the world. (Gn 1,2; Ps 103,29.30) God's spirit came like a force from on high and transformed the great men of old into mighty heroes whom no one could withstand: Othoniel (Jg 3,10), Jephte (Jg 11,29), Samson (Jg 14,6.9; 15,14), Saul (1 Sam 11,6) and Gedeon. (Jg 6,34) Both the ecstasies of the *nabi* and the experiences of the greater prophets are attributed to the mysterious power of God's spirit. (Nm 11,17.25.29; 24,2; 1 Sam 10,6.10; 2 Sam 23,2; Is 11,2; 42,1; 61,1; Ez 3,12.14; 8,3; 11,1.24; 43,5) In fact in the Nicene Creed we profess belief in the Spirit "who spoke through the prophets."

In the New Testament we continue to see all works of God's power as wrought by the Holy Spirit. The angel Gabriel informs Mary that her son will be conceived due to the power of the Holy Spirit. "The Holy Spirit shall come upon you and the power of the most high shall over-shadow you." (Lk 1,35) For this reason her child is referred to as "begotten of the Holy Spirit." (Mt 1,18.20) The Spirit again descends upon Christ at his baptism (Mk 1,10; Lk 3,22; Mt 3,16), leads him into the desert (Mt 4,1; Lk 4,1), and fills him as he returns to Galilee. (Lk 4,14) The Master himself acknowledges publicly that he has the anoint-ing of the Spirit of the Lord, and that it is he who is behind all his works. (vv.18f) "If I cast out devils by the Spirit of God, then the kingdom of God has come upon you." (Mt 12,28) This is the very explanation that St. Peter gives of our Lord's miracles: "You know . . . how God anointed Jesus of Nazareth with the Holy Spirit and with power, and he went about doing good and healing all who were in the power of the devil." (Ac 10,38) It is this power which the Savior promises his disciples: "Wait for the promise of the Father. . . . You shall receive power when the Holy Spirit comes upon you." (Ac 1,4.8) They were to be clothed with power from on high. (Lk 24,49)

THE SPIRIT OF ADOPTION

It has been said that St. Luke, the evangelist of the Holy Spirit, presents us with a diptych whose hinge is Christ's death and resurrec-tion. One panel, his gospel, shows the activity of the Spirit on the humanity of Jesus, whereas the other panel, the Acts, shows that same activity of the Spirit on the followers of the Risen Christ. It is the same Spirit who glorified Christ's human nature, who was showered upon us by that same Christ, and in turn transforms us into Christ's image and likeness.

Once the apostles had been clothed with the power of the Holy Spirit (Ac 1,5; 2,4.33), they went forth into every area of the known world, spreading the kingdom of God always under the intimate direc- 37 tion of the Spirit and with his power. (Ac 8,29; 11,12; 13,2.4; 15,28; 16,6f; 20,28; 21,4) This was the full realization of the Master's promise: "The Advocate, the Holy Spirit, whom the Father will send in my name, will teach you all things, and bring to your mind whatever I have said to you." (Jn 14,26; 15,26; 16,13f)

The Savior's insistence that man must "be born again of water and the Holy Spirit" (Jn 3,5) finds a faithful echo in the teaching of St. Paul. In his writings the Holy Spirit appears not only as holiness itself but also as the producer of that holiness within us. Holiness is love of God by imitation of Christ. The Spirit of Christ brings about within us our divine adoption in Christ: "Whoever are led by the Spirit of God, they are the sons of God. Now you have not received a spirit of bondage so as to be again in fear, but you have received the spirit of adoption, by virtue of which we cry 'Abba! Father!' The Spirit himself gives testimony to our spirit that we are sons of God." (Rom 8,14ff; Gal 4,6) It is by him that the "charity of God is poured forth in our hearts." (Rom 5,5) Or to put it another way, we are sanctified by the Spirit (Rom 15,16; 1 Cor 6,11); he makes us belong to Christ (Rom 8,9), for it is in this one Spirit that "we are baptized into one body" of Christ. (1 Cor 12,13) Though there is a variety of gifts and ministries in the body of Christ, "all are the work of one and the same Spirit." (1 Cor 12,4-11) It is by the Spirit that Christians live. (Gal 5,25) He makes it possible for us to recognize Jesus as the Savior and Lord (1 Cor 12,3); he even prompts our prayer (Rom 8,26), as he makes us into a dwelling place for God. (Eph 2,22; cf.1 Jn 3,24) All this is part of the gradual process of our rising with Christ "by the power of the Spirit who dwells" in us (Rom 8,11), of our being transformed into Christ's very image through his Spirit. (2 Cor 3,18)

Since the role of the Holy Spirit in our sanctification is so universal, the sacraments certainly do not elude his divine activity. It is directly and explicitly affirmed by the sacred writers in the case of baptism (Jn 3,5; 1 Cor 12,13), confirmation (Ac 8,17; 19,6), penance (Jn 20,22) and orders. (Ac 20,28) For St. Paul all sacred ministries are the work of the Holy Spirit. (1 Cor 12,5.11)

Though the Fathers of the Church gave their best attention to baptism and the active role of the Holy Spirit in it, St. Cyril of Jerusalem in his *Mystagogical Catecheses* (3,3) also attributes the efficacy of transubstantiation in the eucharist and the anointings with oil and chrism to the Spirit. St. Augustine sees the Holy Spirit active in all the blessings of the Church. (*Treatise on the Epistle of John*, 3,2) Finally, St. Isidore of Seville aptly summarizes the teaching of the Church when he says: "They [the sacraments] are fruitful when administered in the Church, because the Holy Spirit, abiding in her, hiddenly works the effects of the sacraments." (*Etymologies*, 6,19,39)

In the sacraments, then, we are transformed into Christ by the power of the Spirit; the Spirit forms us in this way into the risen body of the Son of God. We become identified with Christ, but by the agency of his Spirit.

CHAPTER FIVE

"SAUL, WHY DO YOU PERSECUTE ME?"

—Ac 9,4

Few of us are given the marvelous grace which St. Paul received while on his way to Damascus to cast Christians into prison. Proud defender of the Law of Moses, he had in his possession documents authorizing him to punish all who professed faith in the name of Jesus. He never got a chance to use them. He was struck down from his horse and blinded by a flash from heaven. Bewildered, he heard these amazing words:

"Saul, Saul, why do you persecute me?" To his question, "Lord, who are you?" came the straightforward reply: "I am Jesus whom you are persecuting." (Ac 9,4f)

Notice that the Savior did not ask Paul why he was persecuting Christians. Pointedly he demanded: "Why are you persecuting me?" St. Paul understood. In the days and years which followed this moment of his conversion he had much to learn; but all of it was colored by this event—so much so, that once he began to preach the gospel, whatever he had to say was centered on the identification between Christ and the Christian.

It is probable that from the apostles or from other Christians, Paul learned of the Master's beautiful Last Supper address. The message reported in St. John's gospel must have burned through to his heart.

> I am the vine, and my Father is the vine-dresser. Every branch in me that bears no fruit he will take away; and every branch that bears fruit he will cleanse, that it may bear more fruit. . . . Abide in me, and I in you. As the branch cannot bear fruit of itself unless it remains on the vine, so neither can you unless you abide in me. I am the vine; you are the branches. He who abides in me, and I in him, he bears much fruit. For without me you can do nothing. (Jn 15,1–5)

The point of our Lord's teaching here is that his life is brought to us in the context of a community. Those who live his life form one living organism. Branches are not a society which the vine founds and in which it retains a benign interest. Branches simply cannot live unless they are attached to the vine; there is no other life for them except the one life of the vine. At the same time, the vine's life is handed on from one branch to another; each part plays an essential role in the life of the whole, in the other's receiving and maintaining the same life. Christ is the vine on whom we, the branches, live; and it is his life that we live, his life which we hand on to one another.

To insist that Christ's life which we live is not his human life is perhaps to pinpoint the obvious. We already have this life from our parents; we do not receive it from Christ. We can continue to exist humanly quite well without Christ. The community of life about which he speaks here is the life of God flooding his humanity and overflowing into ours. This life we can receive only from him, and only with him can we live it.

THE BODY

This message is central to St. Paul's theology of the Christian life, but it is offered to his readers under a different image, that of the body. "Just as in one body we have many members, yet all the members have not the same function so we, though many, are one body in Christ, severally members one of another." (Rom 12,4f) Or again: "As the body is one and has many members, and all the members of the body, many as they are, form one body, so also is it with Christ. For in one Spirit we were all baptized into one body." (1 Cor 12,12f) He then goes on to show that a body must have many members each having its own function, each necessary to the other and to the whole.

> The body is not one member, but many. If the foot says, "Because I am not a hand, I am not of the body," is it therefore not of the body? And if the ear says, "Because I am not an eye, I am not of the body," is it therefore not of the body? If the whole body were an eye, where would be the hearing? If the whole body were hearing, where would be the smelling? But as it is, God has set the members, each of them, in the body as he willed. Now if they were all one member, where would the body be? But as it is, there are many members but one body. And the eye cannot say to the hand, "I do not need your help"; nor again the head to the feet, "I do not need you." Nay, much more, those that seem the more feeble members of the body are more necessary; and those that we think the less honorable we surround with more abundant honor, and our uncomely parts receive a more abundant comeliness, whereas our comely parts have no need of it. But God has so tempered the body together in due portion as to give more abundant honor where it was lacking, that there may be no disunion in the body, but that the members may have care for one another. And if one member suffers anything, all the members suffer with it, or if one rejoices, all the members rejoice with it. Now you are the body of Christ member for member. (1 Cor 12,14–27)

For Paul, the remarkable thing is not the fact of unity in the body of Christ, but that it must have diversity of members to be a body at all. Since Christ gives us his supernatural life as members of an organism, we need one another's ministrations. Each member must serve the other in the supernatural realm, or God's plan is nullified. Each member con-

42

tinues to receive Christ's supernatural impulse of life and to maintain that vital experience through the agency of other members.

As Paul says in the above text, we have been baptized by the Spirit into one body. Baptism is our birth into this heavenly organism, a birth which reproduces Christ within us—so much so that we must then consider ourselves to have "put on Christ." (Gal 3,27) As a consequence we have become a new creature, a new man in Christ. (Gal 6,15; Eph 2,15; 4,24) That is why St. Paul could glory in the fact that it was no longer he that lived, but that Christ lived in him. (Gal 2,20)

Paul's teaching on Christian marriage also illumines his concept of the Church as the body of Christ. Christ, he says,

> is the head of the Church, being himself savior of the body. But just as the Church is subject to Christ, so also let wives be to their husbands in all things. Husbands, love your wives, just as Christ also loved the Church, and delivered himself up for her, that he might sanctify her, cleansing her in the bath of water by means of the word; in order that he might present to himself the Church in all her glory, not having spot or wrinkle or any such thing, but that she might be holy and without blemish. Even thus ought husbands also to love their wives as their own bodies. He who loves his own wife, loves himself. For no one ever hated his own flesh; on the contrary he nourishes and cherishes it, as Christ also does the Church, because we are members of his body, made from his flesh and from his bones. (Eph 5,23–30)

Though this last phrase seems to be an interpolation, other Pauline texts (1 Cor 6,13–20; 2 Cor 11,2) confirm it to be St. Paul's thought in this instance. We become one body of Christ. He is our head, we his members. We make up one person, one flesh and blood, as in marriage. Christ saves the body and gives it his own life. As Emile Mersch says: "Since that day when he saw Christ in the Church he was persecuting, it seems that Paul could no longer look into the eyes of a Christian without meeting there the gaze of Christ." (*The Whole Christ*, p. 104)

"OF HIS FULLNESS"

Another text of St. Paul, especially when taken in conjunction with others, serves to deepen our appreciation of the mystery of our identification with Christ on the supernatural level. Christ, he says, was given by the Father "as head over all the Church, which indeed is his body, the fullness of him who fills all with all." (Eph 1,22f) This does not mean that the Church presents herself as a final perfection or completion given to Christ; rather, according to the context of the Epistles to the Ephesians and Colossians, the Church is the body of Christ, like a bride, filled with Christ's riches, containing Christ who acts in and through her. The Church is the one filled, not Christ. Paul says explicitly: "In him dwells the fullness of divinity bodily, and in him . . . you are made full." (Col 2,9f) We must note that here St. Paul uses the present tense: the fullness of divinity *dwells* in the Savior's bodily humanity. Since the resurrection, the fullness of God is contained in Christ, not simply for himself, but in such a way that it spreads out to those who have been made into his body. Through Christ, therefore, the divine life is being poured into his body, the Church.

This is the incredible hope of Christians—that the rich fullness of God which Christ contains should *in him* become theirs. But this can never be true of isolated Christians. This comes about only in that "perfect manhood" which results from Christ's activity as head, who fills all things through the ministry of the Church. This ministry is destined by God for the "building up of the body of Christ . . . to the mature measure of the fullness of Christ." (Eph 4,10–13) The relationship of Christ to the Christian is precisely that of head to member of his body. Christ's grace of headship means that he in his humanity is filled with the divine life and power and communicates it to his Church, his body, that she may bring all mankind back to the Father as another Christ. It is God's plan that Christ "fill all things." (v.10) But the agent of that filling is the Church. It is "through the Church" that the Principalities and the Powers in the heavens come to know "the manifold wisdom of God according to the eternal purpose which he accomplished in Christ Jesus our Lord." (Eph 3,10f) In and through the Church all must grow up in him "who is the head, Christ. For from him the whole body, being closely joined and knit together through every joint of the system according to the functioning in due measure of each single part, derives its increase to the building up of itself in love." (Eph 4,15f) Yes, this growth into Christlikeness comes from Christ in the Spirit, but it is through the "functioning of each single part."

44

This much is clear, then: For us as individuals to achieve the new life of God-in-man, to receive a share of divine life, we must become part of an organism already living that divine life. To one who has eyes of faith, the Church is not merely a social grouping of men who think alike religiously, who uphold the same moral laws, who form a religious lobbying force. The Church is built on the God-man, incorporated into him, elevated to his height and filled with his divine power and life. The Church is the body of Christ. St. Paul does not say that the Church is like Christ's body. She is his body. All who enter her become members of the body of the God-man; so intimately are they joined to him and to each other that they participate together in his divine life and glory. It is important to emphasize, however, that a person is a member of this body only if he lives the life of the body and contributes with initiative and responsibility to the good of other members and the common divine life of the whole.

THE CHURCH AS SACRAMENT

The Church is then, like Christ, the sacrament of God's effective presence among men. Rahner calls the Church the "root-sacrament," while Semmelroth applies the term "primordial sacrament" to her. From her and out of her very substance the seven sacraments flow, because she is the body of Christ, a sign and cause of salvation. As the body of Christ she is but the instrument he uses in expressing himself, in continuing his redemptive activity among men. She is the continuation of the incarnation, and her sacramental functions are her God-given means for making the divine presence felt and the divine life lived. The Church is the body of Christ redeeming us; she is the body of Christ at the instant of his death and resurrection.

In his encyclical *Mystici Corporis,* Pope Pius XII discusses the Pauline doctrine of the Church as the body of Christ. Faithfully he echoes the grand vision of the Apostle. He insists that the Church should be called the body of Christ not only because Christ is the head of the Church, but because "he so sustains the Church, and so in a certain sense lives in the Church, that it is, as it were, another Christ." (Par. 66) This means that our

Savior shares his most personal prerogatives with the Church in such a way that she may portray in her whole life, both external and in-

45

ternal, a most faithful image of Christ. For in virtue of the juridical mission by which our Redeemer sent his apostles into the world, as he had been sent by his Father, it is he who through the Church baptizes, teaches, rules, looses, binds, offers sacrifice. In virtue of that higher, interior and wholly sublime communication, with which we dealt when we described the manner in which the head influences the members [Par. 42–64], Christ our Lord brings the Church to live his own supernatural life, by his divine power permeates his whole body and nourishes and sustains each of the members according to the place which it occupies in the body, very much as the vine nourishes and makes fruitful the branches which are joined to it. (Par. 67)

In this way Christ and his Church, "which on this earth as another Christ bears his person, constitute one new man, in whom heaven and earth are yoked together in perpetuating the cross's work of salvation. By Christ we mean the head and the body—the whole Christ." (Par. 93)

If we speak of the Christian's identification with Christ in the Church through the sacraments, we must understand this well. Such an identification does not rob the human being of his individuality. "In a natural body," Pius XII goes on to say, "the principle of unity so unites the parts that each lacks its own individual subsistence. On the contrary in the mystical body that mutual union, though intrinsic, links the members by a bond which leaves to each intact his own personality." (Par. 74) At the same time, our union in the body of Christ is not just a moral union:

> In the moral body, the principle of union is nothing more than the common goal and the common cooperation of all under authority for the attainment of that goal; whereas in the mystical body this collaboration is supplemented by a distinct internal principle which exists effectively in the whole and in each of its parts, and whose excellence is such that of itself it is vastly superior to whatever bonds of union may be found in a physical or moral body. (Par. 75)

What is this intrinsic principle of union between Christ and Christians in his body?

> Essentially it is something infinite, uncreated: The Spirit of God, who, as the Angelic Doctor says, "numerically one and the same, fills and unifies the whole Church." (Par. 75) . . . What lifts the society of Christians far, far above the whole natural order is the

Spirit of the Redeemer, who until the end of time penetrates every part of the Church's being and is active within it. He is the source of every grace and every gift and every miraculous power. (Par. 77)

As the invisible principle uniting and vivifying every member of the Church just as parts of the human body are given life and united and joined one to the other, the Holy Spirit has rightly been called by Pope Leo XIII the soul of the mystical body: "As Christ is the head of the Church, so is the Holy Spirit her soul." (*Divinum Illud*, America Press edition, p. 11) This is but the traditional teaching of the Church so well exemplified in St. Augustine: "What the soul is in our body, that is the Holy Spirit in Christ's body, the Church." (*Sermon* 187)

It is into this intimate union with Christ living in his Church that each sacrament further inserts the Christian. *The sacrament is a permanent and effective sign of Christ which unites, absorbs, assumes the recipient into the organism of his living body, the Church; thus integrated the Christian becomes identified with Christ, one with him in a supernatural, living extension of himself.* While not losing his individual personal identity, the Christian, nonetheless, lives and acts as Christ on the supernatural level by being united to the Church.

THE CHURCH AS MOTHER

As the bride of Christ, flesh of his flesh, the Church begets her Spouse's divine life in us. In baptism we are born into the Church as God's sons, and yet we are born of her as of a mother; in confirmation she strengthens us in her life; by penance she repairs whatever is injurious to the perfect living of her life; in the eucharist she feeds us with the substance of her Spouse.

The sacraments are always actions of the Church. No matter how secretly they may be administered they are always social by nature, for they join us ever more intimately and permanently to a community of life. Take but one example, the sacrament of penance: the darkness and privacy of the confessional should not obscure the sacrament's essentially ecclesial, or family, perspective. The parable of the prodigal son offers a perfect illustration of this orientation. The returning son while still far off is spied by his father. The good man rushes out of the house and

47

falls upon the boy with paternal kisses and embraces. Once the young-
ster admits his guilt and begs for reconciliation, the father shouts orders.
Bring forth the best of robes to clothe my son, sandals for his feet, a ring
for his finger, and the most pointed command of all, kill the fatted calf
and make ready a merry feast. The sacrament of penance witnesses our
father's embrace in his blessing. Once we have admitted our guilt and
sought forgiveness, he gives orders. Bring forth the best of robes for my
son—the life of grace, the "putting on" of Christ; sandals for his feet—
a sign of God's tender providence for our person; a ring for his finger—
a sign of our readmission into a royal race; and then, incredible gesture
of love, the fatted calf is slain—Christ is crucified for our sins and given
to us as food and drink in a family feast. Penance is our reconciliation
with Christ's body, God's family. It is a direct preparation for the
heavenly banquet of divine love in which we feast, as children around
a common father, on the body and blood of our Savior.

Even though redemption reaches the individual human person, it
is fundamentally a social deed in its effect. The grace which sacraments
produce and maintain does not establish a merely individual relationship between the soul and Christ. Each human being receives this
divine life in so far as he is united to Christ's body mystical from which
men drink of his fullness of divinity. It would be outrageous to con-
ceive of communicants as solitary eaters in a restaurant, since they participate in the family meal of God's people. In like manner every sacrament must be considered as integrating us into the common life of
Christ's body. While they are actions of the Church, our mother, sacraments are also and basically the source and origin of the Church. They
form us into the one body of Christ, apart from which we have no access
to the Father, no adoption as his sons.

So much was St. Cyprian taken with this thought that he warned:
"No man can have God for his Father who will not have the Church
for his mother." (*On the Unity of the Church,* 5)

CHAPTER SIX

"SEALED WITH THE SPIRIT"

—Eph 1,13

As members of the Body of Christ, we have received a special consecration of the Holy Spirit. Because of this we are able to give God to one another. As dedicated temples we have been reserved, set aside by God himself to manifest and make known the great deeds of his mercy on behalf of mankind. We are God's chosen people because we have been stamped with his mark which made of us his inalienable property. We

49

are a holy people fitted out with the divine presence and power. Foreshadowed in Israel, achieved in Christ, we are his priestly kingdom used by him to dispense unto the world the fullness of his divine life.

Already at Mount Sinai when God established the covenant with the Israelites, he told them through the mouth of Moses: "If you hearken to my voice and keep my covenant, you shall be my special possession, dearer to me than all other people, though all the earth is mine. You shall be to me a kingdom of priests, a holy nation." (Ex 19,5f) These words refer immediately to the fact that God was calling Israel to a special worship, a form of worship given from above. The members of this nation could stand before God and find favor with him. The institution of the Levitical priesthood is, of course, well known; but the fact remains that the whole of Israel was called to give worship to the true God through its priests. Of all the tribes of the earth Israel was Yahweh's holy gathering of acceptable adorers.

The status of the holy people was nonetheless itself a promise. Though Israel had priests and was considered a priestly people, a greater fulfillment was yet in store for it. The Book of Isaia reminds the nation of this when he repeats the promise in a messianic perspective: "Strangers shall stand ready to pasture your flocks, foreigners shall be your farmers and vinedressers. You yourselves shall be named priests of the Lord; ministers of our God you shall be called." (Is 61,5f) Israel, after all its defections, was to be restored—in a way that escaped the keenest insight of the prophets.

"BEHIND THE VEIL"

Though Israel was a kingdom of priests, dearer to Yahweh than all peoples, her priesthood was severely limited. The ordinary people were restricted to the outer court of the Temple. The priests could minister in the tabernacle. Only the high priest could enter the Holy of Holies behind the veil—and that but once a year with the greatest fear and trembling. The Messia removes this obstacle; he pierces this veil in his own body. (Heb 10,20) He penetrates to the very presence of God once for all (9,11f), and brings us with him: "We are free to enter the Holies in virtue of the blood of Christ." (10,19) Through him we are able to go straight to God (7,25); "we may draw near with confidence to the throne of grace." (4,16)

Throughout the epistle to the Hebrews there is insistence on the superiority of the Christian covenant. Christ's priesthood is continually exalted above the Levitical service, for Christ is sinless, perfect, eternal. (ch.7) The worship of the Old Law priests was "mere copy and shadow of things heavenly." (8,5) But Christ "has obtained a superior ministry, in proportion as he is mediator of a superior covenant, enacted on the basis of superior promises." (v.6) He brings to us the worship of heaven itself.

In consequence, the Christian likewise undergoes a change which renders him superior to those who lived under the Law. Though many were the great heroes of the faith of olden times, "they did not receive what has been promised, for God had something better in view for us; so that they should not be perfected without us." (Heb 11,39f) The Greek word used for this "perfecting" of Christians is *teleiōsis*. It is the same word, as a matter of fact, which serves for the description of Christ's perfect priesthood. (2,10; 5,9; 7,28) Indeed, the word *teleiōsis* is a technical expression employed by the Septuagint translation to refer to priestly consecration. Hence, when Hebrews says that by one offering Christ has perfected forever those who are sanctified (10,14), it is equivalent to saying that Christians were consecrated priests by Christ's sacrifice. Because of such consecration they are able to eat from their altar. This certainly seems to be the sense of the statement: "We have an altar of our own, from which they who carry out the worship of the tabernacle have no right to eat." (13,10) To eat of the altar's sacrifice is a priestly privilege, but the priests of the Old Law cannot eat of the new altar. Besides having a new sacrifice and a new priest, Christ, Christians also must possess a new kind of consecration, a new priesthood given them by Christ.

The great fulfillment of the promises of old has taken place in Jesus Christ. About this St. Peter is quite explicit: "You are a chosen race, a royal priesthood, a holy nation, a people purchased by God to proclaim the great deeds of him who has called you out of darkness into his marvelous light." (1 Pt 2,9) But it is a priesthood which is firmly rooted in Christ. "Draw near to him, a living stone, rejected indeed by men but chosen and honored by God. Be you yourselves as living stones built thereon into a spiritual house, a holy priesthood, to offer spiritual sacrifices acceptable to God through Jesus Christ." (vv.4f) The Christian receives his priesthood only because he is incorporated into Christ. This priesthood enables him to associate himself and his whole life with Christ's sacrifice which alone can make of man's life an act of worship pleasing to the Father.

In the Apocalypse the author portrays this same grandiose vision of the Old Testament prophecies of the incorporation of God's chosen ones into Christ the priest. "And they sing a new canticle, saying: 'Worthy are you to take the scroll and to open the seals; for you have been slain, and have redeemed us for God with your blood, out of every tribe and tongue and people and nation, and have made us for our God a kingdom and priests; and we shall reign over the earth.'" (Ap 5,9f)

Three classical texts of St. Paul are often cited in support of the priestly consecration which all Christians receive. Against accusations of inconstancy and lack of conviction Paul urges the Corinthians to consider the source of his dedication: "The one who stands as warrant for us and for you in Christ is the God who has anointed us and stamped us with his seal and has given us the Spirit as a pledge in our hearts." (2 Cor 1,21f) Though Paul speaks of his personal fidelity to his apostolic mission in this text, it would be a mistake to refer what he says to that mission exclusively. He is merely invoking in his own defense what is true of all Christians, for in another text—in case the universality of the "seal" can be doubted in this instance—he indicates explicitly that all Christians are sealed with the Holy Spirit. "In him [Christ] you too, when you had heard the word of truth, the good news of your salvation, and believed in it, were sealed with the Holy Spirit of promise, who is the pledge of our inheritance." (Eph 1,13f) Or again, "Do not grieve the Holy Spirit, in whom you were sealed for the day of redemption." (Eph 4,30)

In other words, Paul's reference to the "anointing," the "seal," and the "pledge of the Spirit" in 2 Corinthian 1,21f should be interpreted in this way: God has given his fidelity to Paul as well as to the faithful; the immediate source of that divine fidelity is incorporation into Jesus Christ himself, the sacrament of the Father's faithfulness. This union with Christ becomes a reality through the "anointing" and the "stamping with his seal" which makes the Christian Christ's property. To what, then, do these expressions refer? We certainly cannot say that the char-

52

acters of baptism and confirmation are explicitly intended here, but an impressive number of competent exegetes recognize a sacramental atmosphere about the texts cited above, and hold that these characters are definitely implied in what St. Paul says. These texts provide solid foundation for the later distinct doctrine that baptism and confirmation impress an enduring "mark" on the soul, for the very notion of "sealing" or "stamping" implies a permanent effect. Hence the Council of Trent solemnly defined that the three sacraments—baptism, confirmation and holy orders—imprint on the soul a character, which "is a certain spiritual and indelible mark." (D852[1609])

SPHRAGIS

Trent's definition regarding the sacramental characters was but the culmination of a long theological development. And this development began with the theological endeavor of the Fathers. The Greek word for "seal" in the above scriptural texts is *sphragis*. Other words that help translate its meaning are stamp, sign, mark, brand. The Fathers exploit the rich imagery of the term and in this way try to bring out the various facets of the wondrous reality which takes hold of man during the sacraments of initiation.

First, they point out that through this "signing" a man becomes the property of Jesus Christ, is incorporated into his flock. Just as sheep are branded to indicate their owner, so the Christian is marked in order that his belonging to Christ be accompanied by a title of possession. Cyril of Jerusalem urges his catechumens: "Draw near and receive the sacramental seal (*sphragis*) so that you may be recognized by the Master. Be numbered among the holy and recognized flock of Christ, so that you may be placed at his right hand." (*Catechetical Lectures*, 1,2) He even calls baptism "the holy and ineradicable seal." (*Procatechesis*, 16) Theodore of Mopsuestia has the same point of emphasis:

> This sign with which you are now marked is the sign that you are from now on marked as a sheep of Christ. For a sheep, as soon as it is purchased, receives the mark by which its owner may be known. It also feeds in the same pasture and is in the same sheepfold as the other sheep who bear the same mark, showing that they all belong to the same master. (*Hom. 2 on Bapt.*, 17)

53

In ancient times a young man wishing to enlist in the service of king and country, after proving his physical ability, would receive on his hand a tattoo indicating to which army he pledged loyalty. Cyril follows this tradition when he says: "The inscription of your name has taken place, and the call to enter the campaign." (*Procatechesis,* 1) Even more pointedly Theodore remarks:

> This signing, with which you are now marked, is the sign that you are now marked as a sheep of Christ's, as a soldier of the King of heaven. . . . The soldier chosen for service, found worthy because of his physique and health, first receives on his hand a mark showing what king he is henceforth to serve; so now you have been chosen for the kingdom of heaven, and you can be recognized, when anyone examines you, as a soldier of the kingdom of heaven. (*Hom. 2 on Bapt.,* 17)

Thus, baptism is also the sign of our enlistment in Christ's army. In another place Cyril reminds his disciples: "Each of us comes to present himself before God in the presence of innumerable armies of the angels. The Holy Spirit marks your souls. You go to enlist in the army of the great king." (*Catechetical Lectures,* 3,3) St. John Chrysostom also emphatically assigns this "sealing" to the Holy Spirit: "As the *sphragís* is imprinted on soldiers, so is the Holy Spirit upon those who believe." (*Hom.* 3,7 *on* 2 Cor.)

It would appear that others too were so marked or tattooed. Slaves were marked with the sign of their master. Along these same lines, even devotees of a god were tattooed in order to show their dedication to the service of this divinity; this was equivalent to a consecration to his worship.

But we really do not have to turn to the pages of secular history for means of understanding St. Paul's use of the word *sphragís.* The Bible itself provides sufficient examples of God's marking men. The first episode concerns the fratricide Cain. God marked him so that no man would kill him. (Gn 4,15) Such protection on God's part was not a sign of favor but of punishment—he would have to live with his crime. Other instances of divine protection of men by means of a mark were indeed manifestations of God's favor and predilection. When God was about to deliver the Israelites from Egypt, they were told to mark their doorposts with the blood of the lamb. The Israelites would be recog-

54

nized by such blood, and the plague would not strike them (Ex 12,7.13) Again, in Ezechiel's vision of the future destruction of Jerusalem, he beholds an angel of the Lord marking the foreheads of faithful Israelites with a *tau* which preserved them from the angel of death. (Ez 9,4ff)

Finally, the Book of Apocalypse beholds the glorious vision of the sealing of the elect and their final joyful experience. The judgment of God is again in question here—destruction of the wicked. To protect the just from such devastation God has them marked: "Do not harm the earth or the sea or the trees, until we have sealed the servants of our God on their foreheads." (Ap 7,3) In this case, however, the just are sealed not merely for protection. For in the following verses they are seen as shepherded by the Lamb into glory. They are marked out for glory, signed for participation in the eternal liturgy of heaven:

> After this I saw a great multitude which no man could number, out of all nations and tribes and people and tongues, standing before the throne and before the Lamb, clothed in white robes and with palms in their hands. And they cried with a loud voice, saying, "Salvation belongs to our God Who sits upon the throne, and to the Lamb." (vv.9f)

Indeed, "having washed their robes and made them white in the blood of the Lamb, they stand before the throne of God and serve him day and night in his temple." (vv.14f) Of interest here is a point of grammar in the original text. The verb "sealed" is in the perfect tense in each instance, thus indicating an action with lasting effect.

SEAL OF THE COVENANT

As beautiful as all this imagery is, we have not yet penetrated to the deepest meaning of the seal. St. Cyril of Jerusalem makes another remark which is very thought-provoking. It brings us right to the very center of the meaning of baptism—*sphragís*. He says: "After faith we, like Abraham, receive the spiritual *sphragís*, being circumcised in Baptism by the Holy Spirit." (*Catechetical Lectures*, 5,6) Relating the baptismal seal to Jewish circumcision is of prime relevance, for just as the Jewish rite was the sign of Israel's alliance with God and the means of other men's entrance into it, so baptism is that which seals the new alliance and stamps each new member of Christ with incorporation into his kingdom. The thought that stands uppermost here is precisely the fulfillment of the covenant.

How Pauline is this thought. We have already seen how St. Paul connects faith and the *sphragís* in Ephesians 1,13: "In him [Christ] you too, when you had heard the word of truth and the good news of salvation, and believed in it, were sealed with the Holy Spirit of promise." In another text he uses the same word *sphragís* in reference to Abraham's circumcision: "He received the sign of circumcision as the seal of the justice of faith." (Rom 4,11) The parallelism is so striking that there is no doubt that Paul is constructing a comparison between circumcision and baptism both of which set the seal upon a man's faith. In fact, he also says: "In him [Christ] too, you have been circumcised with a circumcision not wrought by hand, but through putting off the body of the flesh, a circumcision which is of Christ. For you were buried with him in baptism, and in him also rose again through faith in the working of God who raised him from the dead." (Col 2,11f) Indeed, circumcision itself no longer matters, but rather a new creature. (Gal 6,15) In other words, the seal of the old covenant has been perfected and fulfilled by the seal of the new, baptism.

The theology of the covenant has a very important bearing, therefore, on our understanding of the seal or character of baptism. It is of the essence of the covenant that it be an act of God's love by which he obligates himself irrevocably to the one with whom he makes the covenant. Man may sin against God and thus withdraw himself from the divine promise, but the promise itself is never revoked. As something stable, definitive, man can always appeal to it.

For a very good reason, then, the Fathers applied this same idea of permanency to the baptismal *sphragís*. St. Cyril of Jerusalem calls it the "holy and indelible *sphragís*." (*Procatechesis*, 16) In another place he prays that "God give you the ineffaceable seal of the Holy Spirit for eternal life." (*Ibid.*, 17) Like circumcision of old, baptism is a contract with God founded on God's promise of unwavering love. As the seal of the new covenant, baptism places an irrevocable claim on God's love. Fickle man may withdraw himself from enjoying that eternal love, but the contract on God's part remains unshakable. It is an ever faithful engagement on his part toward man, the official seal which makes man a Christian. The character is an extension of the incarnation, an irrevocable agreement with God that the bearer belongs to his Son and has certain rights before the Father.

Neither Paul nor the Fathers formed a distinct and clear doctrine of the character imprinted on the soul by means of the sacraments of initiation. However, among the effects of these sacraments they did recognize a reality quite distinct from grace—a reality which was inviolable and actually incorporated the recipient into the mystical body.

Augustine furthered the clarification of this doctrine about the sacramental character. Until his time some Fathers spoke of the seal of baptism, while others taught that baptism could not be repeated. Augustine brought these two streams of thought together, showing that the permanence of the sacramental character was the reason why the sacrament could not be reiterated. The Donatist heresy, which was the occasion of this theological progression, claimed that heretics and schismatics had to be rebaptized. Augustine drew a sharp distinction between the validity and the fruitfulness of the sacraments. Various councils and popes had condemned the rebaptizing of those who had fallen away from the faith. Augustine argues from this that there must be something permanent about the sacrament. Though grace can be lost through sin, the character cannot. In like manner a valid sacrament will impart the character but not necessarily grace. Because the character is a kind of objective consecration which remains permanently in the soul, it must be recognized when the wayward return to the Church. It is also the source of the saving effect of the valid but fruitless sacrament once the obstacle of sin is withdrawn.

PARTICIPATION
IN CHRIST'S PRIESTHOOD

In the early centuries of the Church theologians did not distinguish too clearly between a consecration which comes from sharing in Christ's life of holiness and that altogether special configuration to Christ's priesthood which is the effect of the sacramental character. The ancient Fathers indeed spoke of the Christian's being marked in a particular way as belonging to and being like Christ. St. Augustine definitively established the permanent quality of the sacramental character. How-   57 ever, it was due to the genius of St. Thomas Aquinas that this sacramental character finally came to be seen as a share in Christ's priesthood operative in the sacramental life of the Church, not just a priesthood expressing itself in terms of personal acts of holiness and apostolic dedication.

Thomas explicitly refers many of the biblical texts which we have quoted to what we may call the priesthood of holiness. The royal priesthood spoken of in the epistle of Peter, for instance, has as its immediate foundation the Christian's sharing in that effect of Christ's redemptive work called sanctifying grace. The spiritual sacrifice to which the Christian must be devoted by reason of his living in and with Christ is the sacrifice of a moral life, the practice of virtue. The baptized Christian enjoys a spiritual union with Christ through faith and charity and therefore is in possession of a spiritual priesthood. (*S.Th.*, 3,82,1, ad 2)

Yet, St. Thomas clearly sees another title to priesthood in Christians in addition to grace itself. He says:

> A character is properly speaking a kind of seal whereby something is marked as being ordained to some particular end. Thus a coin is marked for use in the exchange of goods, and soldiers are marked with a character as being deputed to military service. Now the faithful are deputed to a twofold end: first and principally for the enjoyment of glory, and for this they are marked with the seal of grace. Secondly, each of the faithful is deputed to receive or to bestow upon others things pertaining to the worship of God. And this deputation properly comes from the sacramental character. Now the whole rite of the Christian religion is derived from Christ's priesthood. Consequently it is clear that the sacramental character is especially the character of Christ. The faithful are configured to his priesthood by reason of the sacramental characters, for they are nothing else than certain participations in Christ's priesthood, flowing from Christ himself. (*S.Th.*, 3,63,3)

This last type of priesthood, Aquinas clearly states, refers not to grace, but to the actions belonging to divine worship. (3,63,4 ad 1) He admits indeed that grace is given to man as an aid in carrying out worthily actions of worship to which he is deputed. But grace is not the primary concern of the character. While all the sacraments produce grace and thus make man a participant in Christ's priesthood (as receiving an effect of that priesthood), only three sacraments imprint a character on the soul which deputes man to do something or to receive something as he engages in Christ's own worship as priest. (3,63,6 ad 1)

Clearly, then, we have two specifically distinct ways in which we participate in Christ's priesthood: one of sanctifying grace, the other of the sacramental character. The first we rightly call "priesthood of holiness," for the simple reason that throughout Christian tradition, both biblical and patristic, the notion of sacrifice extended far beyond public, ritual, or liturgical sacrifice. St. Augustine summed up this tradition well when he defined sacrifice as "every good work done with the aim of uniting oneself to God in holy fellowship." (*The City of God,* 10,6) The performance of good works, the practice of asceticism and virtue proper to a member of Christ was clearly an exercise of Christ's priesthood of holiness.

The second kind of priesthood, that of the sacramental characters, is more restricted in its purpose, at least as envisaged by St. Thomas. He continually speaks of the sacramental character in the context of "rite" or "divine cult," and says explicitly that the "rite of the Christian religion is derived entirely from Christ's priesthood." (3,63,3) His thinking, therefore, is definitely of the social, institutional, public, sacramental, liturgical order—a sacrificial order of a specific type with Christ himself as the sole true priest. The Christian's share in this unique priesthood is precisely to enable or empower him to engage in Christ's own priestly worship in his Church—a worship of God which has, rightly and ultimately, Christ as the responsible person and effective power behind it.

St. Thomas calls the sacramental character an instrumental power. (3,63,2, and 5 ad 1 and ad 2) But this must be correctly understood. We have already seen that the sacraments are *signs* of Christ's saving work in his Church. The precise function of the sacramental characters is to produce such supernatural, life-giving signs. The character enables the one who possesses it to make natural actions signs of a supernatural transaction. It raises what may seem to be ordinary activities of men to the level of sacramental sign-language; it makes them valid sacramental signs which God uses to produce grace instrumentally. Without such a sacramental character a person could go through the same actions which we call sacraments, but they would not be sacraments. The character secures validity for the acts of the members of the Church in her ritual, particularly in her sacraments. Because of the sacramental character the human body performs or receives sacraments not as natural things, but precisely as valid sacramental signs serving Christ as his instruments of worship and salvation.

A STRUCTURED CHURCH

These sacred seals of baptism, confirmation and holy orders, then, are necessary so that the Church might continue Christ's worship and his redeeming activity among men. These three sacraments which imprint a character are what make it possible for Christ to continue to live on in his Church as the sign of the Father's love and of man's response to that love. Through each character the Christian is more fully incorporated into Christ and therefore into his mystical body; he acquires his place, his role, his function in that body. Endowed with such supernatural power the body of Christians is able to reproduce Christ's own redemptive mystery in contemporary society in the form which he instituted, namely, in sacramental signs. For this reason we say that the sacramental characters are what structure the Church, make it a hierarchical society with each member contributing his part toward the prolongation of the sacred event of the incarnation.

Obviously, each character has its particular purpose. While the whole mystical body is priestly, not every member enjoys the same priestly power. The baptismal character incorporates a human being into Christ and gives him a basic sharing in Christ's priesthood. This priesthood enables the bearer to represent the passive humanity of Christ which needed to be glorified. He does this by receiving the sacraments. His interior dispositions, his faith, his love, his submission enter into the sacramental action as his personal contribution to it, and thus it constitutes the sign of man being redeemed by the paschal mystery. Such baptismal priesthood reaches its height in the celebration of the Mass wherein the one who participates employs his priesthood to designate Christ's sacrifice as the *sign* of his self-surrender to God, of his love, of his desire to be filled with the paschal Spirit, to be divinized.

The ordained priest, on the other hand, by reason of his power serves Christ actively, representing the godhead in Christ redeeming and glorifying fallen humanity. Because of the validity of the priest's actions performed through his character, he receives a further influence from God making of him an instrument to produce the grace-effects of the sacraments. For the ordained priest the character finds its greatest expansion in the eucharist where he makes Christ's paschal mystery present for the Church to share.

Confirmation imprints a character which brings to the baptismal character an enlargement consisting of mature responsibility in the service of Christ. The bearer of such a character now engages in the ritual of the Church with a social perspective. Immersing himself in Christ's paschal mystery, he has an eye to carrying Christ and his redemptive work to those men around him who have not yet been responsive to God's transforming love.

By means of the sacramental characters, then, the Church is an ordered society, an organism, each of whose members possesses his proper function. They are seals which set men apart from the world and assume them into Christ's redemptive mission to that world. As St. Paul reminds the Ephesians, Christ himself gave "some men as apostles, and some as prophets, others again as evangelists, and others as pastors and teachers, in order to perfect the saints for a work of ministry, for building up the body of Christ." (Eph 4,11f) The seals are powers which validate as supernatural before God the human actions men perform in the sacraments, making the sign an efficacious carrier of divinizing action. Indeed, the Church continues Christ because through the sacramental characters she is Christ redeeming mankind.

CHAPTER SEVEN

"HE WHO BELIEVES IN ME SHALL LIVE"

—Jn 11,25

While the sacramental priesthood is essential to the organic functioning of the Church as the body of Christ redeeming the world today, the priesthood of holiness is no less important for the fruitful fulfillment and complete realization of Christ's redemptive work in the hearts of men. God accomplished the salvation of mankind in Christ's redeeming sacrifice and resurrection; such was the deed that achieved mankind's reconciliation with the Father. This saving act is brought to each man in the sacramental life of the Church. Insertion into the redeemed and redeeming body of Christ requires, however, a personal act on the part of each man. God's gift of life demands a positive response in the recipient, for grace can be given only where it is freely accepted.

Our response to the divine gift is made through faith. St. Paul reminds the Ephesians that they were "saved by grace through faith." (Eph 2,8) By faith we give ourselves entirely to Christ's transforming action and accept the stark consequences of dying and rising with him. Faith is not simply an intellectual assent to Christ's preaching. It is a total surrender of ourselves to the paschal mystery, being the commitment of the whole human personality to living the life of the risen Christ.

"IF CHRIST BE NOT RISEN"

Faith's whole impulse is toward God's saving love. It is not centered upon the distant Deity as upon a matter of cold, dispassionate contemplation. God did not reveal himself to man to be known and pondered and dissected by the human mind as a lifeless and untouchable riddle. This was, unfortunately, Aristotle's god—a prime mover who did not know about us and hence could not have cared less. No wonder the Greeks lost interest in such an elusive ultimate force, and returned to the gods of popular religion. The god of the Deists was only slightly better: he knew about us but did not elect to help us, nor did he wish any truly personal relationship with us. The Christian God far outstrips such weak conceptions. He reveals himself in the very act of lifting us up to himself—to his intimate life. He does not bother revealing the niceties of his inner nature; these he leaves for us to deduce from what he does for us. His personal love in human form, Jesus Christ, is the heart of the Christian revelation. This personal love, as it transforms and divinizes us, is the primary consideration of Christian faith.

In a rather terrifying way St. Paul reminds us of this fundamental fact of the Christian life: "If Christ be not risen, then vain is your faith, for you are still in your sins." (1 Cor 15,17) Over and over again in Scripture, faith is connected with the paschal mystery. Justice will be credited to us "if we believe in him who raised Jesus our Lord from the

63

dead, who was delivered up for our sins and rose again for our justification." (Rom 4,24f) "If you believe in your heart that God has raised him from the dead, you shall be saved." (Rom 10,9) "Since we have the same spirit of faith, we also believe. . . . For we know that he who raised up Jesus will raise us up also with Jesus." (2 Cor 4,13f) "If we believe that Jesus died and rose again, so do we believe that with him God will bring those also who have fallen asleep through Jesus." (1 Thes 4,14)

The Master had told Martha: "I am the resurrection and the life. He who believes in me, even if he die, shall live; and whoever lives and believes in me shall never die." (Jn 11,25f) Incredible is the greatness of his power toward us who believe. (Eph 1,19)

The great power of God toward believers is manifested in the person of Jesus Christ. He is the master of life, for he is the "firstborn from the dead." (Col 1,18) The author of the epistle to the Hebrews keeps clearly before us the fact that Christ the Redeemer is the center of our belief, when he urges us to fix our eyes "upon Jesus, our leader and example in faith, who in place of the happiness which belonged to him, submitted to a cross, caring nothing for its shame, and has taken his place at the right hand of the throne of God." (Heb 12,2) The conqueror of death and the giver of life has become Christ "the Lord." (Rom 10,9; 1 Cor 12,3; Phil 2,11) Hearing the Master's extraordinary claim that he was "the resurrection and the life," Martha blurted out the response of faith: "Yes, Lord, I believe that you are the Messia, the Son of God." (Jn 11,27) St. John writes his gospel in order that men may see and hear what Jesus has done so as to "believe that Jesus is the Christ [Messia], the Son of God, and that believing . . . may have life in his name." (Jn 20,31) The fact of Christ's being the Messia, the Redeemer, is essential to faith. He becomes life-giving for the individual person when that person commits himself through faith to the fact of Christ's death and resurrection. This is likewise a commitment to Christ himself as the means of our reconciliation with the Father (Rom 3,25f)

Faith, consequently, does not contemplate primarily the transcendent God. It is wholly taken up with the incredible *event* of God's intervening in human history as he justifies, transfigures, divinizes human nature in Christ. With this saving event, human history and destiny are understandably altered. Man must make a choice—belief or disbelief. Faith opens man's heart to the paschal mystery and allows God to perform that same miraculous transformation in him which he

64

wrought in the human nature of Christ. Through faith we immerse ourselves in the Christ-life. We simply cannot remain what we were.

"COME TO ME
THAT YOU MAY HAVE LIFE"

In every human relationship of love the two lovers must leave their individuality, to some extent, in order to enter into each other and live as one. So, too, when faced with God's invitation of love in Christ, man is forced to leave his self-centered world, his grandiose illusion of self-sufficiency, and come to Christ. He must embrace his life, make it his own. This is precisely what faith does for a man. St. John beautifully describes faith as a coming to Christ. The Master reminds the Jews that the very Scriptures in which they search for everlasting life bear witness to him. "Yet," he complains, "you are not willing to come to me that you may have life." (Jn 5,39f)

After miraculously multiplying the loaves and fishes, our Lord declares himself to be "the bread of life. He who comes to me shall not hunger, and he who believes in me shall never thirst. . . . All that the Father gives to me shall come to me, and him who comes to me I will not cast out." (Jn 6,35.37) Later, after promising the Jews that he would give his flesh and blood as food and drink, he acknowledges: "There are some among you who do not believe. . . . This is why I said to you that no one can come to me unless he is enabled to do so by my Father." (vv.65f) Then at the feast of Tabernacles he cries: "If any man thirst let him come to me, and let him who believes in me drink." (Jn 7,37ff)

This frequent juxtapostion of "believe-come" has profound meaning in St. John's gospel. Faith is a coming into contact with the paschal mystery, for by it man unites himself to Christ from whose "belly" flows the Spirit of the resurrection. (Jn 7,38f) Man leaves aside his trust in merely human effort—and for the Jew, trust in the works and racial privileges of the Law (Rom 9,30ff; Phil 3,9)—and embraces Christ as the sole source of salvation. The Christian recognizes that justification cannot be man's own doing (Rom 3,28; 4,5; Gal 2,16; Eph 2,8f; Phil 3,9), that his own actions can never bridge the abysmal gap that lies between the holiness of God and the weakness of his own human nature. Through faith he surrenders himself to the power of the Father and becomes a captive of the Father's love. (Rom 6,17f; 2 Cor 10,5) By faith man completely renounces self-guidance of his own life, for the wisdom of this world seems as nothing. The Christian gives up all so that, in the words of St. Paul, he "may know him [Christ] and the power of his resurrection and the fellowship of his sufferings; to become like to him in death in the hope of attaining to the resurrection from the dead." (Phil 3,7–11)

Such renunciation of self-sufficiency is a real death to self, for it means giving up what is most certain from a human viewpoint, what is most cherished in an earthly sense. St. Paul was not exaggerating when he compared faith to a sacrificial oblation (Rom 15,16; Phil 2,17), for it lays open to God's coming what is most private and inviolable in man. For this reason it is an efficacious personal association with Christ's death and resurrection. Faith means the death of the "flesh," the death of the weakness springing from human pride and self-centeredness; it also means the awakening of the paschal Spirit in man, the conquest of God's love. For Paul, "to live in faith" (Gal 2,20; 3,11; Rom 1,17; cf. Heb 10,13) is to live in Christ or to have Christ in oneself. (2 Cor 13,5) It means to submit oneself so totally to the inner power of Jesus Christ that one can say with St. Paul, "It is no longer I who live, but Christ who lives in me." (Gal 2,20)

Faith is far from being what naturalistic-minded men might call "an enjoyable experience." It is nothing short of terrifying in its consequences. St. Paul presents "living by faith" as a struggle with oneself (2 Cor 13,5), a combat with the forces of darkness. (1 Thes 5,4–8; Eph 6,16; 1 Tim 1,18f) It may even be called a self-defying acceptance of God's transforming word (Rom 4,19f)—not merely a theoretical assent to God's truth, but one which issues in and works by charity (Gal 5,6), one that elevates every area of human existence (vv.13.26.) A Christian who truly means his commitment of faith will ultimately have to admit with Paul: "With Christ I am nailed to the cross." (Gal 2,19)

"UNLESS THE FATHER DRAW HIM"

While we insist on faith as one's personal surrender to God's grace, we must not miss the point of what our Lord says. "No one can come to me unless the Father who sent me draw him, and I will raise him up on the last day." (Jn 6,44) Though faith is a truly personal act on the part of the believer, it is nonetheless an effect of God's operation in the soul. It is his call—his drawing of the soul to Christ—that gives rise within the believer to his adherence to Christ and his way of life.

Paul is no less definite on this score. His very description of God's plan of redemption shows this.

> We know that for those who love God all things work together unto good, for those who, according to his purpose, are saints through his *call*. For those whom he has foreknown he has also predestined to become conformed to the image of his Son, that the Son should be the firstborn among many brethren. And those whom he has predestined, them also he has called; and those whom he has called, them he also justified, and those whom he has justified, them he has also glorified. (Rom 8,28–30)

To acknowledge Christ as the Savior requires faith. Pointedly Paul reminds the Corinthians that even this is possible only by the power of the Holy Spirit: "No one can say 'Jesus is Lord' except in the Holy Spirit." (1 Cor 12,3; cf.v.9)

More explicitly he insists that faith is a gift: "By grace you have been saved through faith; and that not from yourselves, for it is a gift of God." (Eph. 2,8; cf. Gal 5,22) Paul gives thanks that the Thessalonians received the word of God from him: "You welcomed it not as the word of men, but, as truly it is, the word of God, who works in you who have believed." (1 Thes 2,13) On Christ's behalf Christians "are given the grace not only to believe in him but also to suffer for him." (Phil 1,29) In fact, from beginning to end, from the seeds of faith to its full fruition, in every aspect of the Christian life—all is a divine action on man: "It is God who of his good pleasure works in you both the will and the deed." (Phil 2,13; cf. Rom 12,3) Man is moved by God at every moment of his salvation—freely, of course, but still efficaciously.

Faith, then, is not only man's personal gift of himself, his opening of his heart to Christ's death and resurrection, but a part, a product of the paschal mystery. A man can recognize Christ as the Redeemer only in the Spirit; yet we must remember that the Spirit himself is a paschal gift. Not only does faith have the paschal mystery as its primary objective; it is itself an effect of Christ's redemptive work. Though faith is man's response—an absolutely necessary one, at that—to the divine

67

initiative, that faith still remains a creation of God's eternal purpose in view of the merits of Christ.

TOWARD THE UNITY OF FAITH

For St. Paul faith is not purely an individual union with Christ. As personal as it is, like everything else in the Christian life, it too has its ecclesial aspect and orientation. Faith is a response to the common vocation of mankind. In Chapter Five we have studied the sacraments as functions of the Church, as the continuation of the body of Christ redeeming man. The sacramental priesthood of all Christians finds its ultimate basis in this same supernatural reality. No less does the priesthood of holiness, and the faith upon which it rests, situate itself in this same context.

First, generally speaking all of St. Paul's writings breathe this social atmosphere. Both the prologue and conclusion of practically all his epistles insist on the communal nature of Christianity. He often begins by saluting the faithful of a given church as sharers in the common good and destiny of the followers of Christ, a design of the Father for man's salvation carried out by the power of the Spirit in the humanity of Jesus. In his conclusions he usually utters a prayer for their continued fidelity to their commitment to growing in, propagating, and making more resplendent to the eyes of men the Christ-life of the one body of the Savior.

The faith, then, of which the apostle Paul so often speaks, must be seen against the general fundamental background of his concept of the Christian life. In this light faith becomes an allegiance to Christ, not as an historical heroic figure of the distant past, but as he is contained in the Church. Belief brings a man into the supernatural organism which lives, breathes and radiates Christ. Through this act of adherence the newcomer attaches himself to the redeemed humanity of Jesus Christ and in turn becomes one with others who live of that glorified body and lend themselves actively to be agents of its continuous redeeming and witnessing role in the world.

More specifically, Pauline teaching takes great pains to show that faith in Christ has made Christians one with all the heroes of faith in the Old Testament. (Heb 11,1—12,2) All nations of the earth are united as one because of faith, for men of faith "are the real sons of Abraham," as God had foretold to Abraham because of his faith: "In you shall all nations be blessed." (Gal 3,7ff) Indeed, Abraham has become the father of all believers. (Rom 4,11f)

Such spiritual union as between father and sons is also enjoyed by the apostle himself, for he speaks of Timothy, Titus and Onesimus as his sons in the faith. (1 Tim 1,2; Tit 1,4; Phlm 10) All that Paul suffers is for his offspring in the faith. (Cf. 2 Cor 4,8–15; 1,6f) In the same way, those who belong to the faith must be imbued with a Christlike fraternal devotion for each other: "Let us do good to all men, but especially to those who are of the household of faith." (Gal 6,10)

Moreover, faith tends essentially toward unity. Paul urges the Ephesians to walk worthy of their calling, using as their motto: "One Lord, one faith, one baptism." (Eph 4,1–5) His whole work of ministry is precisely for the "building up of the body of Christ until we all attain to the unity of faith." (vv.12f) The Old Law divided and separated men; the faith of Christ has made all one.

> Now that the faith has come, we are no longer under a tutor. For you are all children of God through faith in Christ Jesus. For all you who have been baptized into Christ, have put on Christ. There is neither Jew nor Greek; there is neither slave nor freeman; there is neither male nor female. For you are all one in Christ Jesus. And if you are Christ's, then you are the offspring of Abraham, heirs according to promise. (Gal 3,25–29)

Faith, then, is our self-surrender to Christ's work in us in baptism, in which he makes us his one body.

It is this same dynamism of faith that impels Christians to collaborate actively in extending the kingdom of Christ. Paul praises the Thessalonians for having imitated him and the Lord in receiving God's word in such a way as to become a pattern to all believers in Macedonia and Achaia. "For from you the word of the Lord has been spread abroad. . . . In every place your faith in God has gone forth." (1 Thes 1,6ff) He tells the Philippians how much his sufferings have given courage to others "to speak the word of God without fear," and he exhorts them to remain "steadfast in one spirit, with one mind striving together for the faith of the gospel." (1 Thes 14,27)

Preaching the word is not enough, however; faith urges us to propagate the gospel in a way that is even more self-involving. Each Christian, once he has joined himself to Christ by faith, must begin to live for other Christians, for they are Christ. St. Paul's beautiful description of how the body of Christians must work together points to the fundamental way in which men give Christ to one another. Proportionately as we are committed to Christ in faith, we experience in every fiber of our being the burning desire to serve him in his members. Just as each member of a human body needs the other members, just as all of them must work together in harmony for the good of the whole, so all Christians must "have a care for one another. And if one member suffers anything, all the members suffer with it, or if one member glories, all the members rejoice with it." (1 Cor 12,25f) This common living of the Christ-life, as in a body in which each member serves and loves the other, is the basic means whereby the believer bears witness to the transforming love of the Father in Christ through the Spirit. As the old adage goes, "Words teach, example attracts."

"ONE LORD, ONE FAITH, ONE BAPTISM"

Varying emphases in Paul's writings may mislead us into attributing too exclusive an importance to one point or another. His insistence on God's eternal plan of predestination in Christ, for example, may lead some into thinking that all mankind is automatically saved in Christ. Such a conclusion would be preposterous, for the whole weight of Pauline teaching stands against it.

A more intricate problem is to evaluate the relationship between faith and the sacraments. One might be led to believe that justification comes only by faith in Christ. (Cf. Rom 3,22–30; 10,9.10.13 etc.) But then he would forget that it was also Paul who reminded Titus that God "saved us through the bath of regeneration and renewal by the Holy Spirit." (Ti 3,5) Neither can it be claimed that Paul saw some kind of magic power in the sacraments of the Church, as though man could be sanctified by receiving the sacraments without any genuinely personal involvement. The simple fact is that, to speak only of baptism, three-fourths of Paul's baptismal texts clearly and explicitly insist on the important role faith plays in sacramental operation. Faith and the sacraments are two realities which are not just closely allied, but are in fact inseparable in producing the Christ-life.

70

Echoing the simple command of the Master, "Go into the whole world and preach the gospel to every creature. He who *believes* and is *baptized* shall be saved, but he who does not believe shall be condemned" (Mk 16,16), the author of the epistle to the Hebrews places faith and baptism side by side among the basics of Christian doctrine (Cf. Heb 6,1f.) In the epistle to the Ephesians faith and baptism are again found united, consecrated by the "name of the Lord" as a basis for fulfilling the same vocation and causing the union of Christians in the one body of Christ under the Spirit. "Be careful to preserve the unity of the Spirit in the bond of peace: one body and one Spirit, even as you were called in one hope of your calling; one Lord, one *faith*, one *baptism*, one God and Father of all, who is above all, and throughout all, and in us all." (Eph. 4,3–6) Without further explanation at this point Paul simply presents the two as converging means for realizing our heavenly vocation. The same is true of 1 Corinthians 15,14, and 29: Faith and baptism both bear on the resurrection of the Lord and on the resurrection of his followers.

In other texts Paul definitely teaches that faith exercises a real effectiveness in sacramental sanctification.

> We were buried with him [Christ] by means of baptism into death, in order that, just as Christ has arisen from the dead through the glory of the Father, so we also may walk in newness of life. . . . But if we have died with Christ, we *believe* that we shall also live together with Christ. . . . Thus consider yourselves as dead to sin but alive to God in Christ Jesus. (Rom 6,4.8.11)

The future tense, "shall live," does not refer merely to bodily resurrection from the dead, for verse 11 makes it clear that Paul is speaking here of the new Christian life already begun.

While the reference to the role of faith in this resurrection to the . new life is somewhat veiled in this passage, it becomes very explicit in a parallel text in Colossians: "You were buried together with him in baptism, and in him also rose again through *faith* in the power of God who raised him from the dead." (Col. 2,12) Faith, then, is at least a condition for the interior flowering of the grace of baptism.

We must go further. Faith is more than an indispensable prerequisite for a fruitful sacrament. It exercises a true and real causality in our justification and sanctification. God's redeeming power is at work interiorly through faith. Therefore faith complements baptism and the other sacraments, which are the power of the saving love of God in external, visible form.

There is no doubt that Paul ascribes a primary and inherent efficacy to the sacraments. He reminds the Galatians that they are the children of God through faith in Christ Jesus, "for all you who have been baptized into Christ, have put on Christ." (Gal 3,26f) It was in the "bath of regeneration" that God saved us. (Cf. Ti 3,5) In baptism we have been "washed . . . sanctified . . . justified in the name of our Lord Jesus Christ and in the Spirit of our God." (1 Cor 6,11) We are "cleansed from an evil conscience by sprinkling" and by having "the body washed with clean water." (Heb 10,22) "In one Spirit we were all baptized into one body." (1 Cor 12,13)

Nonetheless a man must approach the sacrament with "a sincere heart in fullness of faith." (Heb 10,22) Faith precedes the sacrament, for by faith we are enabled to see Christ as the source of salvation, we place our trust and confidence in him, we come to him. Only this disposition allows us to open our heart to his influence and consummate the movement toward divinization by "being baptized into him." (Gal 3,27)

Faith also works in and follows the sacrament, insuring its effect. In baptism Christians give themselves to Christ by an act of the will. They become Christ's and crucify their flesh with its vices and concupiscences. (Gal 5,24) Not only, then, does the sacrament put to death the "old man," but we also have the believer producing this result consciously as he gives himself, through faith, to God's operation in the sacrament. This is truly *human* cooperation with God's working, but it is not parallel with the divine power, for God inspires and produces faith in man. Granting that faith is a grace of God, we must admit that man willingly puts himself at God's disposal and submits through faith to Christ's dying and rising within him by means of the sacrament—a process that is continued by living in the Spirit by faith. (Cf. Gal 5)

"I AM THE BREAD OF LIFE"

St. John expresses this same relationship between faith and the sacraments in his account of the Lord's promise of the eucharist. Our Savior begins his discourse by placing together faith and sacramental eating: "I am the bread of life. He who comes to me shall not hunger, and he who believes in me shall never thirst." (Jn 6,35) He then insists on the absolute necessity of faith in anyone who would enjoy his divine life. "This is the will of my Father who sent me, that whoever beholds the Son and believes in him, shall have everlasting life, and I will raise him up on the last day." (v.40.)

Jesus then goes on to require an actual eating of his flesh and a drinking of his blood.

> I am the bread of life. . . . This is the bread that comes down from heaven, so that if anyone eat of it he will not die. I am the living bread that has come down from heaven. If anyone eat of this bread he shall live forever; and the bread that I will give is my flesh for the life of the world. . . . In very truth I say to you, unless you eat the flesh of the Son of Man, and drink his blood, you shall not have life in you. He who eats my flesh and drinks my blood has life everlasting, and I will raise him upon the last day. For my flesh is food indeed, and my blood is drink indeed. He who eats my flesh and drinks my blood, abides in me and I in him. As the living Father has sent me, and as I live because of the Father, so he who eats me shall also live because of me. (Jn 6,48–58)

Yet he returns to his insistence on the necessity of faith: "It is the spirit that gives life; the flesh profits nothing. The words that I have spoken to you are spirit and life. But there are some among you who do not believe." (vv.64f) Christ gives himself, the bread of life; man must assimilate it by adhering to Christ in faith. This very adherence is expressed by eating the sacramental flesh and blood of the Redeemer. The nourishing power is in the bread, Christ's body. With faith man eats the Lord's body and allows its power to take hold of him.

"SACRAMENTS OF FAITH"

Just as sacraments are instruments of the Church giving birth to the divine life in men, so are they vehicles bearing the desire of her members to be transformed into Christ. In either case they are signs of faith. Sacraments are sensible signs denoting and producing a holy interchange between God and men, *the* holy interchange: Jesus Christ, man glorified with divine life. This is the whole object of faith—salvation in Jesus Christ, who summarizes in himself man's self-surrender to

73

God and God's gift of himself to man. Whether on the part of the Church or on the part of her members, the sacraments are signs of this faith.

The faith of the Church intervenes first in the sacrament, insuring its internal value, giving it a divine meaning and efficacy. She is, after all, the household or commonwealth of redemption; she is the primordial sacrament of Christ himself. She it is who determines the presence of her Spouse and the divine Spirit in the action she performs and thus makes it a channel of the paschal mystery.

The faith of the Christian comes into play in the sacrament too— as son of Mother Church, receiving of her life, allowing himself to be molded into a son of his mother's Spouse. The faith of the member is a share in the faith of the Church—hers creative, his receptive. Each sacrament calls for an ever deeper personal involvement of the Church's members in her living faith, her faith that is life-giving. The fruitfulness of the Christian's reception of her sacrament depends on the depth and vigor of his participation in the Church's faith.

Such a conception of the sacramental life of the Church makes clear how imperative it is that all Christians drink deeply of her life of faith, how necessary that they become imbued with the spirit of her great son, Paul, who counted "everything as loss compared with the supreme advantage of knowing Christ Jesus my Lord. For his sake I have suffered the loss of all things, and I count them as rubbish, in order to gain Christ and be found in him." (Phil 3,8f) If the faith of the member is to be as effective in receiving and growing in the Christ-life as the Church's faith is in producing it, then it must be a faith of well-rounded and deepened conviction that sees with single-mindedness beyond the human veil of men and things and events toward the divine wealth of lasting value, a faith of burning charity which yearns for transfiguration into Christ, a faith of stout hope which overcomes all obstacles—the varied forms of idolatry of modern civilization and the paralyzing sloth from within—to win the prize of God's heavenly call in Christ Jesus (Phil 3,14), a faith of inexhaustible zeal which aches with a passion for the salvation of souls and counts nothing too much in order that all men may know "Jesus Christ and him crucified." (1 Cor 2,2) According to Paul's instructions to Titus, a believer in God should be the first "to excel in good works." (Ti 3,8) Only such a man who lives intensely the 74 sacraments of faith of Christ's body mystical can truly be called, with the twelve, an apostle of Christ and witness of his resurrection. (Ac 1,22)

CHAPTER EIGHT

"LIVING TO MAKE INTERCESSION FOR US"

—Heb 7,25

For all our emphasis on what God does to man through the sacraments we must never forget that the sacraments are our chief way of worshiping God. They are signs of faith—ours and the Church's. As signs of faith they are our God-given means of submitting to his sway, of opening ourselves to his transforming action, of allowing him to make us entirely his own. Signs of faith, the sacraments are our expression of adherence to Jesus

Christ in his eternal act of self-surrender, of return to his Father's love. As such, then, they are definitely acts of worship, the highest possible form of worship, for they are Christ taking hold of us and giving us back to his Father as replicas of himself.

Aquinas points out the twofold aspect of worship. The virtue of religion inclines man to give God the reverence due to his supreme majesty. But this can be done in two ways. Man can show his reverence for God not only in praising him, but also in submitting to his dominion. In either case it amounts to giving God something. In the first, more direct way we give him an open manifestation of our respect and esteem: praise, adoration, thanksgiving, sacrifice. In the second way we give ourselves to him by laying bare our dependence on him: asking something of him—prayer of petition—and receiving his life—sacraments. Through all the acts of the virtue of religion "man protests the divine excellence and his subjection to God either by giving God something or by receiving something divine." (S.Th., 2ª2ᵃᵉ, 81,3 ad 2) Really, worship is much like love. A man can love by giving himself to another directly in making a gift to the beloved of either a deed or a thing. What so many of us do not realize is that we can also show our love for another by accepting a gift from him, letting him see our willing dependence on him.

"I AM THE WAY"

We may be tempted to think that receiving gifts from others carries with it a tinge of selfishness rather than love. This can be true. But in thinking that this is always true, we are very likely influenced by the many examples of aberrant human love in which one or both parties are imprisoned in a child's world of self-seeking, in which they try to get out of the other party all they can—in which, therefore, not love, but selfishness is the influencing factor behind the relationship.

This simply cannot be true of a genuinely Christian understanding of the sacramental life of the Church, if we are to judge it from the viewpoint of Christ, the *Ursakrament* or primordial sacrament, who is not only the source of the seven sacraments, but the model, or prototype, of what they do to men. The sacraments were not intended by God as a magic salve of divine pity for the mere dressing of human ills; they are the paschal mystery bringing the glorified likeness of Jesus Christ to men. If Christ said, "I am the way," then to live his life means to be like him, to live a life of total surrender to God, to live of God's life—to *be* the Son of God.

We must not think that the sacraments are any less worship simply because they are more immediately directed toward man. Though aimed at man's uplifting, they raise man to God. This is precisely how man best gives glory to God—by belonging to him, by being his, in some sense by being God. What greater act of worship—or love, for that matter—can there possibly be than to become the object of our praise, to become identified with the one we love, to make his life our own? No wonder St. Augustine claimed that "the perfection of religion is to imitate him whom we adore." (*The City of God,* 8,17) This is the very summit of Christian existence from which every action takes its meaning: "the mature measure of the fullness of Christ." (Eph 4,13) In the beautiful ideal of love proposed by our Lord, "No greater love has a man than to lay down his life for his friend" (Jn 15,13), the chief thing envisioned is not biological death but rather the death to self involved in *living for the friend.*

IMITATIONS OF THE SACRAMENTS

Though sacraments are the highest and most efficacious form of the Church's worship, there is yet more. As extensions—or, in the words of the Church, "imitations"—of them, sacramental rites are also part of her integral cult. So similar indeed are they to the sacraments themselves that for centuries theologians made no distinction between them. Sacramentals were simply referred to as sacraments. Peter Lombard (d. 1160) seems, in fact, to have been the very first to use the term "sacramental" when speaking of the ceremonies surrounding the essence of baptism. Others before him simply distinguished between sacraments which are necessary for salvation and those which are not, for example, being sprinkled with blessed water, reception of ashes, funerals, etc.

Imitations have something in common with the original model and yet are different. Like sacraments, sacramental rites are first and foremost sensible signs expressing the unique transforming event of salvation history: the interchange of man's surrender to God and God's gift of his life to man which is the paschal mystery. They also ultimately

77

enjoy the same effective power: the priesthood of the risen Christ and the sanctifying influence of the paschal Spirit.

Yet sacramentals are different. They have been instituted by Christ not directly but indirectly through the decision of the Church. Consequently the paschal mystery is not contained by the sacramentals in the same way as by the sacraments. The effects of the redemptive action are brought to the soul in the sacramentals through the prayer of Christ in his Church. While the sacraments actually contain the saving event, in the sacramentals the graces of that event are prayed for by the Church. Because of her holiness and the priestly power of Christ acting through her, these graces are infallibly made available to men. Just as in the case of the sacraments, of course, the recipient or user of sacramentals must be properly disposed to receive the graces offered by God because of the Church's intercession. The more devotion, the more faith, the more resolution that goes into their reception, so much the more will the recipient be seized and reshaped by the paschal mystery.

Sacramentals and the sacramental prayers of the Church, such as the divine office, could only have been instituted by the Church in service of the sacraments. While not belonging to the essential redemptive work of Christ, sacramentals are an entire system of sacred signs and symbols—prayers, exorcisms, blessings, gestures—developed by the Church with Christ's authority to prepare for, accompany, enlarge, and prolong the core of the sacraments. They dispose men to celebrate the sacraments more worthily by removing obstacles to their operation, exciting within the heart a yearning for Christlikeness. The Church uses some sacramentals to set certain persons apart for the worship of God and the sanctification of men—tonsure, minor orders, subdiaconate, the blessing of abbots, the consecration of virgins—much in the same way as she consecrates things to be used in her sacred worship, such as the church building, the altar, the chalice, and the vestments. Her prayerful blessing brings God's grace down upon the infirm to help them live in the spirit of the cross and seek a higher life with the risen Christ. Her blessings help us to carry Christ's redemptive work into the material world about us: crops, food, automobiles—yes, and television! She liberates inanimate nature from slavery to the devil and dedicates it to the service of God. Thus, reducing its power to draw men away from God and making it an image and symbol of the world transfigured and divinized by Christ, she forges it into an instrument for the sanctification of mankind.

78

There is, then, an organic unity in the Church's worship—everything in it is sacramental, that is, sacred sign-language expressing the holy interchange of divine life and human homage or self-surrender. Sacramentals lead us to and help us extend the power of the sacraments into every aspect of our day as we live it. The sacraments have the eucharist as their center and focal point. Baptism, confirmation, penance and holy orders prepare Christians for participation in the Mass, while matrimony and the anointing of the sick (extreme unction) increase and intensify our hold on the paschal mystery which we renew in the most perfect way during our celebration of the eucharist. The eucharist, then, stands at the very heart of the Church's worship, of the entire Christian life. As the "end and consummation of all the sacraments" (S. Th., 3,63,6), it most expressively and completely continues the redemptive incarnation of the Son of God.

"ASK THE FATHER IN MY NAME"

The Church's worship is acceptable in God's eyes because it is nothing else but Christ's worship of his Father; it is Christ's worship in and through his body mystical. As we have seen in Chapter Three, the supreme moment of Christ's glorification of his Father was when he surrendered himself to his Father and was accepted by him—the paschal mystery. In virtue of this sublime act of love, Christ, according to the Epistle to the Hebrews, has achieved eternal salvation for his members. (Heb 5,9) "He is able at all times to save those who come to God through him, since he lives always to make intercession for them." (7,24f) He enjoys an everlasting priesthood. (5,6)

This priesthood he chose to share with his members, so that his priestly life would be continued among men without interruption throughout all ages and its saving graces brought to every human being. Quite apart from his having invested certain of his followers with the powers of the hierarchical priesthood, he very clearly wanted the entire Church to join intimately with him in his worship. Did he not say: "Where two or three are gathered together in *my name* there am I in the midst of them?" (Mt 18,20) At the last supper before he was taken captive he reminded his disciples:

79

> You have not chosen me, but I have chosen you, and have appointed you that you should go and bear fruit, and that your fruit should remain; that whatever you ask the Father in *my name* he may give you. . . . If you ask the Father anything in *my name,* he will give it to you. Hitherto you have not asked anything in *my name.* Ask, and you shall receive. (Jn 15,16; 16,23f)

The name of Jesus was indeed an ever-present and pervading reality for the early Church; it summed up the quintessence of Christianity: the person of Jesus Christ living and acting in his Chruch. Peter cured a lame man and acknowledged before the chief priests and elders of the Jewish people that it was in the name of Jesus that he had done so, for "there is no other name under heaven given to men by which we must be saved." (Ac 3,6; 4,9–12) Christians were known as a matter of fact as those "who called upon this name" (Ac 9,21; 1 Cor 1,2), for they had been baptized in the "name of the Lord Jesus." (Ac 8,16; 10,48; 19,5) Paul urged that all be done in the name of Jesus (Col 3,17) and that thanksgiving be constantly given to God through that name. (Eph 5,20; Col 3,17)

The reason for the power of this name, of course, is that it was bestowed upon Christ by the Father as he exalted him high above every creature, making him the source of salvation (Eph 1,21; Phil 2,9ff; Heb 1,4; 5,8f), the channel of access to our heavenly Father (Rom 5,2; Eph 2,18; 3,12; Heb 4,16; 7,25), sole mediator between God and man.

To pray in the name of Jesus, therefore, is to invoke the power of his priesthood, to join our voices to the never-ending intercession which he makes before the throne of his Father, presenting humanity washed in his precious blood to the Father as other sons. Pius XII pointedly stated in his encyclical *Mediator Dei* that "the liturgy is nothing more nor less than the exercise of Christ's priestly function." (Par. 22) Through the Church's liturgical worship his priesthood becomes a "continuous and living reality through all the ages till the end of time." (Par. 22) He insists that such worship on her part is more acceptable to the Father than any other kind of prayer, for "she acts always in closest union with her Head." (Par. 27) "Along with the Church her divine Founder is present at every liturgical function: Christ is present at the august sacrifice of the altar both in the person of the minister as well as under the eucharistic species. He is present in the sacraments infusing into them the power which makes them ready instruments of sanctification. He is

present, finally, in the prayer of praise and petition we direct to God."
(Par. 20) The Church's unique union with Christ the priest in worship
is the reason why she concludes all her prayers with the phrase "Through
our Lord Jesus Christ."

A MYSTERY OF TOGETHERNESS

Christ's priesthood has a marvellous power of welding people together; because of it we, though many, go to God as one—as Christ.
Nowhere is the Church more one than in her worship. Pius XII defined
the liturgy as the

> public worship which our Redeemer as *Head* of the Church renders
> to the Father, as well as the worship which the *community* of the
> faithful renders to its founder and *through* him to the heavenly
> Father. In short, it is the *integral* public worship of the Mystical
> Body of Jesus Christ, Head and members. (*Mediator Dei*, 20)

In her liturgical worship the Church acts as one, since everything
she does is done precisely as the action of the one body of Christ with
him as Head, as priest. This is why Pius XII was able to say: "The contribution of the hierarchy as well as that made by the faithful in the
liturgy are not to each other as two separate quantities, but they represent
the collaboration of the members of the same organism which acts as a
single living being." (Address to Assisi Congress of Pastoral Liturgy,
September 1956: *Assisi Papers*, 226) Christ's priesthood, present and
active in the members of his body, is so essential that without it there
could be no liturgy. Though in our personal, private prayer lives we go
to God as individuals—never of course divorced from the body of Christ
or his priesthood—in the liturgy we act as the *one* people of God in its
proper condition of the divinely chosen holy cult-community, the single,
unified expression of the priestly movement of Jesus Christ back to his
Father.

Liturgical worship is a very special kind of worship. That is why it
bears the special name liturgy. Of Greek derivation, it means "work of the
people"; *érgon* means work, while *leîton* means people's. The latter Greek
word is the root of our modern term *laity*. Thus liturgy is the doing of   81
God's holy people. It is not the business simply of the ordained priests;

it is the affair of all members of God's family. Ordained priests as ministers of Jesus Christ, acting in his name, are simply the instruments of the whole mystical body, of each and every member in it. When the priest or qualified layman acts in the name of the mystical body, then the whole body acts as a unit, as the earthly, visible expression of Jesus Christ's worship of his Father.

Just as the ordained priest enjoys a special interior power to act as the agent of the mystical body, so the layman, by reason of his baptismal priesthood, is qualified to participate in its worship—to perform *part* of liturgical cult. As we have seen in Chapter Six, the sacramental character of baptism enables the Christian to enter genuinely into the production of the sacred sign-language of sacramental worship, to lend his words and actions, natural though they may seem, to Christ as an integral piece of his divine glorification of his Father. Such worship produced by the power of Christian priesthood shared by all the baptized, while human in expression, is divine in origin, reality, and acceptability before the Father, because he sees and hears all men as the voice of his only-begotten Son.

All liturgical prayer, then, precisely because Christ's priesthood exercised in the Church is central to it, is essentially social and communal. Since all the members of the mystical body are intimately united to Christ in his priesthood, every liturgical action is eminently common to all of them. Every member of the Church is necessarily involved and affected by such actions. Even if a priest were to recite the divine office alone without any outward manifestation except the movement of his lips, all the members of the Church would pray through him. If the Mass were to be celebrated in the darkest corner of a concentration camp with no one present but the celebrating priest himself, every Catholic throughout the world would be offering through him what he consecrates. This is a tremendous reality. Whether we advert to it or not, we are acting in and are affected by every single liturgical act performed anywhere in the world. No other action of man can lay claim to such awe-inspiring breadth. A liturgical prayer is truly the common act of the mystical body, held and shared, done and enjoyed by every man made child of God through baptism.

The dignity of the sacred assembly at liturgical worship, then, is no small thing. No matter where held, no matter how small, no matter how uneducated, the congregation assembled about its priest for worship is the concrete realization of the mystical body of Jesus Christ. It is the organ of the entire mystical body, expressing its union with its Head in his most sublime role as mediator between God and man, glorifying God in the most perfect way and saving mankind in the most efficacious way.

Each and every member of the congregation is sacred, for each brings to the liturgical celebration a power of priesthood, holy and real according to his condition, which makes of the worship of the group a genuine earthly image of the eternal liturgy of Christ in heaven. The word "image" here does not mean something merely symbolic or figurative. Symbols and signs are indeed used, but this congregation *is* Jesus Christ glorifying his Father in heaven—here under the veil of human time and circumstance. Every Christian contributes to the full actualization of Christ's presence and his prayer. For the complete realization of the mystical body at prayer, no participant may be ignored or counted as unimportant. The priest-celebrant's activity alone will suffice only for "validity" but not for the perfection of the sacramental sign which the Church is. Just as the head is not the whole body, so the image of the Head of the mystical body is not the entirety of Christ. If we want to have all the grandeur of sacramental-liturgical worship, we must find the whole mystical body in visible operation.

The hierarchical and community character which belongs essentially to every liturgical action must be externally seen and put into practice. A grandiose theology of sacramental worship is not enough so long as it remains pure theory. We are in the realm of the sacramental, therefore of concrete sign language which is meant in fact to communicate the salvific event to human beings on their terms—not to teach a notion. The full and active participation of the whole body of the faithful is the primary and necessary source from which they draw the true Christian spirit. (Cf. Pius X, *Tra le sollecitudini,* 3; Vatican Council II, *Constitution on the Sacred Liturgy,* I, 14) Since liturgical functions are not private actions but celebrations which pertain to the whole body of the Church, which is the sacrament of unity, the Church officially desires that their communal celebration—with the full active participation of the faithful—be observed as something preferred over what we might call a "private" use of these functions. (Vatican Council II, *ibid.,* 26 and 27) After all, the laity—not only the clergy—exercises a true active liturgical role by virtue of the baptismal priesthood of its members. (*Instruction on Sacred Music and Liturgy* of 1958, 93,b) What the Church's ordained ministers do in the name of all the members belongs to the members by right.

This organically ordered worship in which each worshiper contributes his share is well provided for in the actual arrangement of the liturgy. The priest-celebrant and his ministers speak God's word to his people. The faithful respond to the divine message by joining in the prayers and songs of adoration, praise, and thanksgiving led by their ordained representatives; they then receive the word of God's sacraments from their hands. In this way a constant dialogue between priest and people runs through divine worship. Even at the most sacred time of the Mass, the preface-canon, the faithful are invited to lend their full-hearted vocal support to what the priest says and does. The action begins with a greeting, "The Lord be with you," addressed to the people, and intimate union between priest and faithful is expressed with the response, "And with you too." To the celebrant's admonition, "Lift up your hearts to the Lord," comes the faithful's clearly convinced answer, "That is why we are here," When urged to give themselves generously to what he is about to do as he cries out, "Let us give thanks to the Lord our God," they agree, "That is the right thing to do." A few moments later they interrupt his praying in their name with the song of the angels, the *Sanctus.* Finally, when the priest has finished the sacred action of the canon, the faithful manifest their willing involvement in what he has done by shouting "Amen." ("We mean it as well as you.")

This basic dialogue pattern pervades the entire liturgy. It is something we must achieve fully—both interiorly and exteriorly—because of what we are: one organic body of Christ engaged in the most important action of that body. In fact, the Church insists that each worshiper take his proper part in her liturgy and do only those things which belong to his role. The celebrant should do and say only what is his priestly part in the service and not take away from the faithful what really belongs to them. Neither should altar boys or choir substitute themselves for the congregation and rob it of its rights.

A FAMILY MEAL

84   As should be expected, of all liturgical functions the Mass is the most social in its arrangement. Since it is the most perfect sacrament of

the paschal mystery, the Savior chose for it a design that discloses exquisitely the intimate meaning of that mystery. Its basic sign language is part and parcel of the fund of human religious expression. While we find the sacred meal used in the worship of almost all religions of the world, it was of paramount importance, in fact the original form of worship, among the Semites. Christ accepted this ready-made cult pattern of the Old Testament and completed it by the divine intervention into human history for which God had prepared it, namely the paschal event.

Yes, the Mass is a meal. Primitive Christianity knew but two names for the Mass. St. Paul calls it the Lord's Supper (1 Cor 11,20), while in the Acts of the Apostles it is referred to as the "breaking of bread." (Ac 2,42) It was, after all, during the Passover meal that the Master instituted the Mass. Mark tells us that

> While they were eating, Jesus took bread, and blessing it, he broke it and gave it to them, and said, "Take; this is my body." And taking a cup and giving thanks, he gave it to them, and they drank all of it; and he said to them, "This is my blood of the new covenant, which is being shed for many." (Mk 14,22–24)

Our Lord consecrated the bread and wine as part of a sacred meal, and he used for this a blessing or eucharist—the grace spoken over food during the meal.

The word eucharist means thanksgiving, grace said over food, a table blessing. Though altered through history, that Passover thanksgiving prayer is found today in the preface and canon of the Mass. It is spoken over food, the bread and wine on the altar. The altar itself is simply a table, consecrated indeed, but still a table. Finally, around the table a community eats and drinks. The picture thus presented is clear. The offertory—misnamed, unfortunately, for nothing is truly offered at this point of the Mass—may be compared to the setting of the table, the preface-canon to the table blessing, and communion to the eating of the food. The basic form of the Mass, then, is a meal, with the bread and wine changed into the body and blood of the Redeemer. This is not simply a symbolic meaning read into the ceremonies of the Mass; the fact that Christ specially chose food for symbols of his body and blood and in his words of institution directly related the eucharist to the Passover meal indicates that he purposely willed this meal character as the sign language for his act of redemption.

The meal in this case is indeed symbolic; it is the sign of friendship and love. At a meal two or more persons show their willingness and desire to unite their lives as they share with each other that which sustains human life. Hence an atmosphere of intimacy, a spirit of communion, dominates the scene. In the same way the Semites used food, a meal, in their attempt to establish a bond between themselves and God, thus entering into intimacy with him. Through rites of offering they acknowledged the victim to belong to God and then sat down with him at table, there to partake of the victim returned to them laden with God's life. Among the Hebrews sacrifice was almost synonymous with eating and drinking before Yahweh. The idea basic to all this was that a victim consecrated to him drew all who fed upon it into the orbit of divine life and holiness. Israel was a nation united within itself and wedded to Yahweh because it sat at table with its God.

In particular, the paschal meal, the most important of Old Testament worship, created a union between God and the chosen people. It was essentially a memorial-meal which effectively brought that original Passover into the very midst of the Jewish family. As they ate this meal the Jews could relive mystically, sacramentally, the events of the deliverance and exodus from Egypt. At one and the same time they became contemporaries of their forefathers, were saved with them, and were brought closer to the messianic fulfillment of that prophetic deliverance.

The Passover meal was a family feast; according to Jewish law it was supposed to be eaten within the family circle. If this were not possible, then a pious group of friends called a ḥabûrah would assemble, one of them taking the place of the father of the family. Following long-established custom, the father would begin the ceremony, in response to the youngest child's query about the meaning of the feast, by reciting the Haggadah, a narrative relating the meal and its various elements to the first Passover. After God's great deeds in favor of his people have been recounted, the father leads his family in the re-enactment of the meal proper, blessing each morsel of food before it is eaten and speaking the concluding solemn eucharist which is a recital of those same saving acts of God in prayer form. All the while the members of the family actively show their personal involvement in the family's salvation by responding to the prayers and joining in the chanting of the psalms.

Three parts make up this celebration: the *Haggadah,* the account of the original Passover and exodus; the *berakah* or blessing, thanksgiving, the grace at the meal; and the actual re-doing of the event in sign, the eating of the meal. Here is the Mass in its most obvious components: Foremass (Mass of the catechumens), the narrative of God's words and deeds; Mass of the faithful, the Christians' grateful response of thanksgiving which sacramentally re-enacts the paschal mystery, subdivided into the consecratory preface-canon—the grace at the meal—and communion, the eating of the divine food.

At the last supper Christ and his apostles formed a *ḥabûrah.* By his novel actions which fulfilled the Old Testament prophetic meal and inaugurated the messianic kingdom, he became the father of a new family. In it, his apostles represented all the children who would throughout history be born unto the Father in baptism. Christ substituted himself for the paschal lamb and commanded his disciples to do the same thing as *his* memorial—not just as a remembrance of him, but as a sacramental reliving of his "once for all" deliverance of mankind. The New Testament writers saw clearly that the eucharist was the Lord's way of allowing the apostles to have a share in his transfigured humanity.

Nowhere better than at the family meal does the father unite his children to himself. This is his greatest opportunity to form his children to his own image and likeness. What he has done in procreating them is minor compared to the immense task that remains of forming within them a personality and goodness representative of his family ideal, and of winning them to his heart as one with him in willing affection. At the family meal he makes his chief manifestation of love toward them by feeding them. The food he places on the table is, when we consider it rightly, his own flesh and blood, for he is in fact the breadwinner. Through his work, tears and sweat—yes, his life—he sustains the life of his family. He thus places himself on the table out of love to be the food of life for his children, and in his table conversation he brands their minds and souls with the stamp of his own personality. The children, on the other hand, in willingly accepting food from the father's hand demonstrate their loving dependence on him, on his strength, on his life. Desirous of living from him, of living his life, they listen to his conversation, eagerly take in these flashing glimpses of his soul; in turn they open their souls to him in their conversation, and allow the formative influence of his paternity to work deeper within them. Here at the family meal is the family created, made one living, cooperating replica of the father.

The Mass is the family meal of God's children. In Jesus Christ, the sacrament of his presence and love, the Father places himself on the table, inviting and warmly welcoming mankind into the embrace of his paternal love. The purpose of the eucharist is to produce and solidify within us a genuine relationship of sons to God our Father. It was not without reason that St. Augustine called the eucharist "a sacrament of filial piety, a sign of unity, a bond of love." (*Commentary on John,* Tract 26,6) In partaking of the body and blood of Christ, we show our love for the Father, desiring to live his life as his only Son.

Just as all those who partook of the communion sacrifices of the Old Testament were drawn into the same sanctification as the victim, so in this eucharistic meal the believer takes possession of the resurrection body of the Savior, receives divine life from the victim of Calvary transformed by God in the resurrection. Christ's passage from death to life now becomes the believer's as he *becomes* the resurrected body of Christ, another son of the Father. Yes, the eucharist creates the Church, for through it each and every member of the Church re-experiences Christ's death and resurrection, dies and rises with Christ to the Father's life, becomes the transfigured Christ as he eats of his transfigured body. We become like God, are effectively changed into his children, his family. God not only invites us to a banquet of love, but places his own body and blood upon the tables as our food. As we engage in this sacred meal, we share food with our Father, life with him. But since the food we share is his flesh and blood, the life we share is his life. Thus does the sacrament of the eucharist effectively symbolize what it was instituted to bring about—intimacy with God, such that we achieve that new state of existence, divine sonship. We become one with the Father in life and love.

There is table conversation too, as befits a family meal. God speaks to his children his word of transforming love in the readings, ("lessons") and gospel of the Mass. We, his children, reply with loving hymns and psalms. Then, with a song in our heart, we set the table at the offertory. Attending to the powerful word of our Father as he blesses the food, changing it into himself, we enthusiastically acknowledge our dependence on him. The first word spoken by the children once grace has been said is quite natural: In the Our Father we ask the Father for bread. We continue our table-talk as we eat, for during the reception of communion we sing from the depths of our soul and thus reveal to the Father our innermost being, asking him to come within and mold us into replicas of himself.

A family affair. Social throughout! The Church is fashioned here; the members of the mystical body are constituted, in Christ, other sons of the Father. How can any Christian, understanding what takes place in the assembly of God's people, withdraw into his isolated world of "My Jesus"? This is like the modern American disease, the TV-tray. Can we call it a family meal when each member takes what he wants from the table and then settles in hardened silence, effectively cut off from the rest of the family, before boxed entertainment?

It does indeed require sacrifice to live with others, for others, as one family under God. But the Mass, we must never forget, is a sacrificial family meal. Each member of the mystical body must continue that original submission he made at his baptism if he is to become the son of God. A sign of love is not enough; this can be illusory. It must be proven through sacrifice. We want to sacrifice ourselves the more for one we love in proportion as we love. As the Father gave all, in Christ, to us, so we must make as complete a self-surrender as possible to his love. As Christ is the sacrament of the Father's love to us, so is he also the sign and bearer of our yielding to that love. If we want the God-life in the risen Christ to be ours, we must achieve in ourselves that same total gift of self which Christ made to the Father on the cross. Immediately after the consecration we say very pointedly: "Wherefore, being mindful of Christ's blessed passion, resurrection and ascension, we offer. . . ." This means that our part in the Mass will be sincere and meaningful only insofar as we let Christ's work of redemption take place within ourselves, only insofar as we place ourselves on the altar of the cross and let the Father transform us into members of his Son. It costs something for a son to let himself be educated into an image of his father. This is precisely the sacrifice we offer at Mass. We raise Jesus Christ to his Father as if to say, "This is what we are; this is what we want to be." Into this symbolic gesture we must pour the full costs of sacrifice involved in dying to ourselves, in casting off the uncleanness of our sinful inclinations, of rejecting individualism. We give ourselves to the Father as the *one* Christ, not as many.

Paul was not speaking metaphorically only when he said: "Because the bread is one, we though many, are one body, all of us who partake of the one bread." (1 Cor 10,17) "We, though many, are one body in Christ" (Rom 12,5), for "It is no longer I that live, but Christ lives in me." (Gal 2,20) When the apostle reminds us that "As often as you eat this bread and drink the cup you proclaim the death of the Lord until he comes (1 Cor 11,26), it is because in the eucharistic sacrificial meal we have nailed ourselves to the cross with Christ (Gal 2,19) and have been filled with the divine life of the Savior, having become his resurrected body and awaiting our final ascension.

All this St. Thomas Aquinas has beautifully summed up in his antiphon for the feast of Corpus Christi. "O sacrificial banquet, in which Christ is eaten, his passion commemorated, and our souls filled with grace and given a pledge of heavenly glory!"

"UNTIL HE COMES"

Transformation into Christ does not come about in a day. If it did, Christ need never have commanded his apostles to celebrate his memorial repeatedly. We all know well enough how genuinely fragile is our hold on the supernatural life, how powerful the enticements of the flesh, how alluring the glitter of the world. Man is made of flesh as well as spirit. Unfortunately, because of original sin the flesh often "lusts against the spirit, and the spirit against the flesh." (Gal 5,17) The two are in open conflict in their desires, and we know which wins out the more often. It was not without reason that our Lord foretold that his kingdom would be like a field filled with wheat and cockle (Mt 13,25f), or a net cast into the sea gathering both good and bad fish. (vv.47f) If we were not in constant danger of weakening and losing the life of paschal newness, to what purpose was his stern warning: "Watch, for you know neither the day nor the hour." (Mt 25,13) Or again:

> Let your loins be girt about and your lamps burning, and you your-selves like men waiting for their master's return from the wedding, so that when he comes and knocks, they may straightway open to him. Blessed are those servants whom the master, on his return, shall find watching. . . . You must be ready, because at an hour that you do not expect, the Son of Man is coming. (Lk 12,35–40)

90 The true follower of Christ must proclaim in his every action, at every moment, "the death of the Lord until he comes." (1 Cor 11,26)

But there is much to reshape in us; our weak wills require a slow process of constant re-exposure to the paschal mystery that will enable them to overcome an excessive attachment to the things of this earth and win complete victory for living in the Spirit. This is why the Church has extended her celebration of the paschal mystery over the entire year. The liturgical year is the Church's means of leading her children toward complete Christlikeness together, bit by bit, in the steps of their elder Brother.

Christ has redeemed time along with everything else. As one from outside time, he lived in time, worked in time, died in time, in order to bring man from time to eternity. Like a constant who fails not, Christ stands at the end of man's past and effectively joins to it the hope of a glorious future. He gradually reshapes man in the course of his cyclic natural life from what he was to what the Father wants him to be.

Though there is some truth in the ancient concept of time as circular—even the modern rectilinear idea of it—the Savior combines both. With him time becomes a spiral. While men remain enmeshed in the same recurring cycles of natural phenomena, each ring of time lived with Christ takes them higher, until they reach the Father's mansion. The Lord has sanctified time, making it a symbol or sacramental of spiritual regeneration, growth, maturity. The Church, using the natural rhythm of the "circle of the year," has constructed a system of feasts and seasons to insert the glorified Christ into man's life. Christians, living together the rhythm of the Church's life, are caught up gradually into the mainstream of Christ's mystery and bit by bit transfigured into his image.

Another way of saying this is that in the spiritual life there are no resting-places; man must either advance or retreat; he cannot remain static. The liturgical celebration of the mystery of Christ, though always essentially the same, confronts man according to different aspects in the various seasons and forces him to take another step, makes him change pace, challenges him to try harder to climb the spiral of supernaturalized time that leads him to permanent union with Christ.

It is of great importance, however, to realize and to insist over and over again that, while it follows the course of nature, the liturgical year of the Church is not a naturalization of the sacred. Christianity is a supernatural religion based upon an extraordinary divine intervention in man's time which lifts him out of time to the everlasting instant of his eternal home. Just as in the case of consecrated things such as wine, water, bread, oil, so the Church's use of time is a divinization of the natural: time is used to transmit the supernatural event of redemptive incarnation. Every feast of the Church is a commemoration of the saving event that happened among men to transform man into God.

We must emphasize again the fact that Christ's priesthood is just as necessary to the vitality and reality of the liturgical year as it is to the sacraments, for the liturgical cycle is nothing less than the sacraments— specifically the Eucharist—working wonders in time in the maternal bosom of the Church.

The commemoration of the work of redemption in the liturgical feast is not a cold and lifeless review of the mysteries of Christ's life or a bare record of a former age. We are not interested in, and certainly do not celebrate, Christ as an historical figure. As everything else in the Church's liturgy, her annual festal observance is *sacramental*. In the Church year Christ represents and renews his life precisely as a way of salvation, the achievement of a very real, intimate union of us with him- self, the glorified human Son of God—the very end and essence of the Christian life.

To say that the liturgical year is sacramental is to say basically that throughout its celebration the redemptive work of Christ is made present. It is not a meditation on his edifying life. Neither is it a series of group Bible-reading sessions.

First: The Church's official observance of the liturgical year is a genuine priestly proclamation of the word of God. When the various lessons and gospels of the seasons are announced to God's people, Chris- tians are not going through the mere formality of paging through Scrip- ture. Special men, equipped with the ministerial power of priesthood through a commission from Jesus Christ himself, stand before all mankind and herald the coming of the kingdom of God. In performing such a func- tion the Church's ministers are not different from the apostles themselves. It is Christ who through them preaches the effective and unchanging will of the Father to reconcile men to himself. This means that right here and now the Father through his sacrament, his Son, is offering mankind his union of love with himself. Men are "called together"—the meaning of *ecclesia*—to hear the words of God himself inviting them to be his people, to accept the challenge of stable fidelity to his love.

God's words are not always the same, something obvious enough when we consider the different phases of the liturgical year. Yet, varied

92

though the expression may be, the same fundamental appeal shines through: "Be my people—be my Son—live my life." Or, to use the inspired expression of this invitation: "Arise, make haste, my love, my dove, my beautiful one, and come; for the winter is now past." (Ct 2,10f) Paul speaks of the same intimate union of love to which we are called when he compares the Church to the bride of Christ. (Eph 5,25ff) Note, we are all called to belong to the one bride of Christ for whom he delivered himself, the one bride who makes but one person with him. Regardless of the particular aspect of the work of redemption being celebrated, the paschal mystery is what is proclaimed.

Second: In her communal spiritual life the year through, the Church obtains for her children by the power of her priestly prayer the grace to welcome into their hearts the divine saving event. As Pius XII says so clearly, "Holy mother Church, while proposing for our contemplation the mysteries of our Redeemer, asks in her prayers for those gifts which would give her children the greatest possible share in the spirit of these mysteries through the merits of Christ." (*Mediator Dei*, 165) The sacramental prayer of the Church—Christ speaking through her to the Father—infallibly brings its effect; the grace of the mystery commemorated is always made present and available for us to take or leave.

Third and most important: The saving event of the redemption itself becomes present, for the liturgical year consists primarily in the celebration of the eucharistic renewal of the paschal mystery. We have already seen how the Lord instituted the Eucharist to make present his original unique salvific act. In fact, this doctrine is enshrined in the secret prayer for the ninth Sunday after Pentecost: "As often as this commemorative sacrifice is offered, there is wrought the work of our redemption." Hence, at each feast of the liturgical year we do not merely behold a picture of our heroic Savior, nor hear a lesson in Christian doctrine, but rather we experience a vivid and real actualization of Christ in his eternally permanent act of redeeming mankind, gathering and forming men into his Father's family, infusing into them the life of his Spirit.

Even though during the course of the year we celebrate the mysteries of Christ's life individually, we must not think that each one of them is made truly present in our liturgical commemoration. Only one historical salvific act breaks the bonds of time and becomes truly present, and that is the paschal mystery: Christ's sacrifice and its acceptance by the Father in the resurrection.

93

Breaking up the one, essentially indivisible redemptive act of Christ into its component parts during the year is only a device permitting us to contemplate more minutely the great mystery of salvation and to drink more deeply of the life of the Spirit released in that mystery. In itself the Christian mystery is much too vast for the human mind to grasp and the human will to absorb. The pattern of cycles and feasts allows us to be introduced slowly, gradually, humanly into the details of the infinite mystery, just as the whole mystery, epitomized in Christ's sacrifice and resurrection, was unveiled to man piecemeal: the incarnation, the preaching the advent of the kingdom, the institution of the sacraments, the drama of the passion as distinct from the resurrection, the marvel of the ascension as separated from the resurrection in time, and the outpouring of the Holy Spirit fifty days later. All these are still part and parcel of the Easter-event of man's salvation.

St. Leo reminds us of this fact when he says: "Among all the feasts held sacred by Christian devotion, none is more excellent than the paschal feast. All other solemnities of God's Church find their dignity consecrated in it." (*Sermon* 48) Easter is the very basis of the liturgical year as well as the oldest of its feasts. The entire year has its climax in the Easter Vigil. The readings and ceremonies of this service have as their obvious theme our incorporation into Christ through his work of redemption. Behind the paschal candle, symbolizing the risen Christ, we follow the transfigured God-man in pilgrimage from the darkness of sin and death to the light of life and freedom. The magnificent *Exsultet* is a glorious hymn of praise to the

> night which became radiant as day . . . the truly happy night which alone deserved to know the time and the hour in which Christ arose from the world below . . . the night which frees from the vices of the world and the dark haze of sin all those who believe in Christ, the night which restores us to grace and the fellowship of the saints.

Before the paschal sacrament of baptism is conferred, or at least before we renew ourselves in the spirit of our baptismal innocence, the original Old Testament events prophetic of our redemption are proclaimed anew to us. Finally we usher in the day of salvation with the sacramental re-enactment and reoffering of the great deed of redemption, the eucharistic sacrificial meal, the Mass.

94

Holy Week is the immediate preparation for this "night of nights."

Beginning with Palm Sunday and running triumphantly through Good Friday—which seems to many a lugubrious day—the fulfillment of Old Testament messianism unfolds in the very midst of God's chosen people, the Christian assembly, sweeping them along in the entourage of Christ the priest-king, who as suffering prophet achieves victory over sin and death. It is a week-long commentary on those momentous words of Jesus: "O foolish ones and slow of heart to believe in all that the prophets have spoken! Did not the Messia have to suffer these things before entering into his glory." (Lk 24,25f)

Lent, our spiritual springtime, is a more lengthy conditioning of the Church so that she can rise in full flower with Christ, rejuvenated by the power of baptism and eucharist, the two paschal sacraments par excellence. A rigorous asceticism is urged upon the Christian in the hope that in this way he will be able to loosen the hold that concupiscence, sin, and inordinate attachments exercise over him, preventing the free movement of grace within him. Prayer and fasting dilate his heart and make way for the operation of the Spirit. This personal, individual asceticism and penance are consecrated and made quasi-sacramental by the Church's communal spiritual life during these days. Each Mass during Lent has been assigned its proper text with themes harking back to the practices of penance and mortification of the pre-baptismal catechumenate, and the administration of the sacrament of penance, of ancient times: instructions concerning the truths of faith and moral duties, exorcisms which drive out the devil, Old Testament types of baptism, sackcloth and ashes, excommunication for sin (symbolically denoted by the veiling of the images in the church during Passiontide, a remnant of an earlier practice of stretching a veil across the entire front of the sanctuary), the need for almsgiving and fasting.

Such points of reference force the faithful to realize the connection between their personal asceticism and that of the Church's communal life, and make them see it as a demand of the baptism they have received and the sacraments of penance and eucharist which they continually approach. All is placed in the perspective of the social paschal event they will celebrate at the great Easter Vigil. Man cannot rise with Christ to the new life of his body in the Spirit unless he is willing to die to himself, to crush his selfishness, to leave his self-centeredness and seek God in love.

The joy and overwhelming importance of Easter impelled the

95

Church from earliest times to extend her celebration for a full fifty days, and though we today call this festive season Paschal Time, early writers refer to it simply as *Pentecostes* or *Quinquagesima*—the fifty days as opposed to *Quadragesima*, the Latin name indicating the forty days of Lent. In pre-Christian times, of course, this season was the Jewish festival of weeks bearing the same name, Pentecost.

During paschaltide we, the Church, relive the experiences of the apostolic college receiving final instructions from the Master. We hear Christ speak of his plans for the Church, of himself as the Good Shepherd leading his sheep, of his going to his Father and sending his Spirit. The last three Sundays of the season take their gospels from the Lord's discourse at the last supper. In them the magnificent reality of our common union with Christ is laid bare dramatically with its trying consequences here below and its grand finale in the eternal home of the Father:

> I am the vine, you the branches. . . . You shall weep and lament, but the world shall rejoice. . . . You too are to be my witnesses. They will expel you from the synagogues. . . . Ask the Father in my name. . . . Now I am going back to him who sent me. . . . If I go, I will send him [the Advocate] to you. . . . One day I will see you again, and your heart shall rejoice, and your joy no one shall take from you. (Jn 15,5; 16,20; 15,27; 16,2.23.5.7.22)

The climax of the fifty-day celebration comes with the feasts of the Ascension and Pentecost. On the first we see our humanity raised to the highest heaven in the person of Jesus Christ; we celebrate the final outcome of the work of redemption, our glorification before the throne of the Father through Jesus Christ. Though we must wait as individuals for our ascension, this feast reminds us that heaven is already ours in Christ. Aptly St. Leo sums up the meaning of this mystery:

> The ascension of Christ is our own exaltation, and whither the glory of the Head has preceded, thither the hope of the body is also called. Let us, therefore, rejoice, dearly beloved, with due gladness. For today not only have we been confirmed as possessors of paradise, but in Christ have we even penetrated the heights of heaven, having gained far more through the ineffable grace of Christ than we had lost through the malice of the devil. For those whom the virulent enemy cast down from the happiness of their first estate, these the Son of God has placed as one body with himself at the right hand of the Father. (*Sermon 75, On Pentecost*)

To insure our progressive ascent to reunion with our Head in heaven, Christ sends upon us his Spirit. Though it is essentially a part of the paschal mystery, we celebrate the outpouring of the Holy Spirit as described in the Acts of the Apostles, fifty days after Easter.

> As the days of Pentecost were drawing to a close, they [the apostles] were all together in one place. And suddenly there came a sound from heaven, as of a violent wind blowing, and it filled the house where they were sitting. And there appeared to them parted tongues as of fire, which settled upon each of them. And they were filled with the Holy Spirit (Ac 2,1–4)

With this startling event Christ begins to act through his Spirit in the apostles, in his Church, in you and me, to bring the rest of mankind out of the misery and death of slavery to the devil. They "began to speak in foreign tongues, even as the Holy Spirit prompted them to speak," to herald the Word of God: the Word of God in preaching, the Word of God in sacrament, the Word of God in their communal Christian living.

Though of later introduction into the Church's system of feasts commemorating the mystery of Christ, Christmas is nonetheless important. Its importance stands out particularly in that its cycle shows an evident attempt to imitate that of Easter. It opens with a period of preparation called Advent, which in some places was named the Lent of St. Martin because it began on his feast day (Nov. 11) and lasted for forty days, Sundays excluded. The climax of the cycle enjoys a night celebration of Mass. Finally its theme is echoed for some forty days until February 2.

The theme of the cycle is obvious enough: a celebration of the coming of the "Sun of Justice" into the world to begin the redemption of mankind. The Church is not interested, however, merely in the earthly birth of a man; she consistently sees him as Savior of men, the light and life of the world. Nevertheless, she pointedly emphasizes throughout the cycle his real manhood, leaving no doubt that the future Savior saved us in and through a genuine human nature. Born of a woman in a lowly condition, he shows himself ready and willing from the first to give up all earthly honor and comfort for the achievement of his goal: surrender of our humanity to the Father to be glorified in a lasting, heavenly life.

97

The Eastern counterpart of Christmas, Epiphany—though histori-cally this should be expressed in reverse—is also celebrated in the Western Church, but its theme is not the birth of the Savior as a human being. Rather, it is concerned with the manifestations of Jesus Christ as divine love and power welcoming all men into his bosom. In addition to com-memorating the coming of the non-Jewish magi, which showed Christ's kingdom to be universal, the Church delicately inserts ideas into the feast which place the whole cycle in a manifestly social and paschal perspective. In the antiphon for the *Benedictus* of Lauds she has us sing: "Today the Church is joined to her heavenly Spouse because Christ washed her crimes away in the Jordan, the magi run with gifts to the royal nuptials, and the wedding party is gladdened with the water made wine." Christ's baptism in the Jordan is seen as imparting to the waters of the earth the special power of the paschal mystery, while the allusion to the marriage feast of Cana expresses the mystical nuptial of Christ with all men in the Church because of which, through the waters of baptism, she is able to give birth to new sons of the heavenly Father.

Some authors consider Advent, and for a greater reason Christmas, as celebrating the *parousia* of Christ. But it is difficult to see how this can be true. The *parousia* has not occurred in its fullness as yet, and the liturgical year commemorates only historical events pertaining to the saving mystery of Christ. We must remember that every feast of the year contains a threefold perspective: past, present, and future. A Christian feast is first and foremost a commemoration of the redemptive work of Christ in one or another of its facets. The immediate aim of this re-membrance, of course, is to draw the assembly of God into the saving event with the ultimate purpose of leading the Church closer to the coming of Christ in glory. Many of the texts of Advent which some invoke in favor of a principal *parousia* theme are quite normal in their place; we find them throughout the liturgical year as a reminder of things to come. However, the gospel for the first Sunday of Advent and St. Gregory's homily on it are definitely not in their proper place. St. Gregory's homily itself indicates that the gospel section was chosen be-cause of its application to a passing event in the city of Rome during his day—a terrible calamity—and entered the missal for this day as a per-manent choice only centuries later. It did not belong to the original Roman Mass text.

The Advent liturgy today has an atmosphere of sorrow and penance. But this was not always so. Originally, the Roman liturgy knew nothing of an Advent fast; that came into existence only around the thirteenth century and was dropped still later. Today the *Gloria* and *Te Deum* are not sung during Advent. But this practice came into the Roman observance of Advent only after the twelfth century.

When we take into consideration the whole of the Roman Advent liturgy, we see that it is possessed of a holy enthusiasm and a profoundly joyful expectation of the coming celebration of the Savior's birth. Any trace of sorrow is really foreign to the heart of our Advent celebration. We find rather an air of exultant happiness—especially we the redeemed —over the tidings brought to Mary, and in this spirit prepare with her for the coming of the Son of God.

The festivals of the saints need no justification for a Catholic. The holiness of the saints is celebrated out of a twofold motive: They are models that encourage us on our way to heaven, and as friends of God their prayers can obtain God's help for us in our spiritual needs. More than in any other case, we must be particularly aware that in feting the saints we are really celebrating the Easter event, rejoicing over the fact that the paschal mystery became so perfectly operative for our forebears in the mystical body.

St. Ambrose sums up this idea beautifully.

> We celebrate the birthdays of the martyrs to announce the glory of the Lord's resurrection to those who were companions to this passion. We announce the paschal grace to the holy martyrs: while their bodies are laid in the tomb and grow cold, their spirit is already warmed by the heat of immortality. (*Sermon* 61, *On the Birthdays of Martyrs*)

The birthday he speaks of is the day on which the saint was born into eternal life, the day of his death on which Christ's ascension took place in him.

As a matter of fact, so deeply ingrained was this attitude in the minds of Christians of early times that only martyrs enjoyed a liturgical cult. No other holy people were so honored—not even the Virgin Mary. Only in the fourth century did authorities begin to realize that men and women who had led exemplary lives here below had lived a lifelong

martyrdom and were more than worthy of the Church's official veneration. Confessors and virgins—mostly those who had lived in the religious
life—were soon honored with liturgical feasts.

The mother of Christ received liturgical recognition for the first
time in the fifth century, as far as history records. Popular veneration
of her took hold quickly after her assumption into heaven, but the im-
petus behind the initiative to celebrate liturgical feasts in her honor seems
to have been the direct result of the definition of her divine motherhood
by the Council of Ephesus in 431. Thus, all her feasts venerate her role
in man's redemption as the mother of God—of God the Savior of men.
She is thus honored precisely as the image of the Church, as mother of
God in the hearts of men. Daughter of the Church, most perfectly
transfigured by the paschal event, she symbolizes in a supreme way the
mystical body of Christ, redeemed by him to redeem other men.

"REFLECTING THE GLORY
OF THE LORD"

Sacramental worship is the spiritual life of the Church. How can
the spiritual life of the Christian be any other than hers? She is his
mother. Unless he allow her to educate him, how shall he become like
his Father?

Man cannot sanctify himself. Try as he will with all his asceticism,
mortification, and prayers, he cannot mold himself to God's image and
likeness. The transformation desired here is divine; it must be performed
by a divine person. God's domain is beyond man's reach. With all our
modern slogans about "zestful living," "every day in every way I'm growing better and better," and our having the biggest and the best of everything here in America, we succumb so easily to naturalism in religion,
making it revolve about human qualities of personality, cleverness,
energy, and organization. How we judge the value of religious per-
sonalities by success in a worldly sense! Who in our culture would dream
of a garbage collector as a saint?

While man certainly has power of his own with which to improve
himself, he cannot bridge the abyss that separates him from God. God
alone can make of us a supernatural race living by the power of grace.

100

That transforming grace comes only through Christ and his redeeming body, the Church. Where else does one find the resurrection body of the God-man?

Through his Church, Christ works the miracle of man-made-over-into-God. And we? We must be humble enough to see ourselves for what we are, lay ourselves open to his sacred action, invite it, cooperate with it. St. Paul understood this well. "All of us, with faces unveiled, reflecting as in a mirror the glory of the Lord, are being transformed into his image from glory unto glory, as through the Spirit of the Lord." (2 Cor 3,18)

This is not to say that human effort is not required in the super-natural life; quite the contrary. God will not violate the privacy of a man. His cooperation is essential to the success of the "divine love affair." While Pius XII reminds us that "if the private devotion of individuals were to neglect the august sacrifice of the altar and the sacraments, and to withdraw them from the stream of vital energy that flows from the Head to the members, it would indeed be sterile" (*Mediator Dei*, 32), he also insists that if the sacramental life of the Church is to produce its proper effect, "it is absolutely necessary that our hearts be properly disposed." (*Mediator Dei*, 31)

The history of spirituality, insofar as it developed apart from the liturgy, is full of oddities. The prayer of the individual is in constant danger of losing sight of the theocentric and of becoming the projection of his own notions and desires. Without a conscious tie with the universal values of the Church's prayer, the prayer of individuals and groups inevitably becomes the prey of sentimentalism and emotionalism and isolationism. The result could not possibly be other than an unhealthy, unbalanced, if not downright uncatholic spiritual life.

No sane approach to the spiritual life can deny the absolute neces-sity of mental prayer (we do not mean the formal meditation according to any particular method), for without reflection on the truths of faith and the event of redemption one cannot give himself wholeheartedly to the divine operation, build up convictions strong enough to attach him irrevocably to a love, imitation, and service of Christ. Mental prayer—the whole of a Christian's life—needs to feed upon the wholesome ob-jective truth of revelation as proposed and interpreted by the Church. Otherwise, instead of bringing man out of himself—educating him—and leading him to the supernatural goal of Christlikeness, mental prayer will only tend to falsify religion, shape Christ to his way of thinking, naturalize Christ.

Consequently Pius XII vigorously warns that forms of private prayer and popular piety are to be condemned, "if they are an obstacle to the principles and norms of divine worship, or if they hinder them or oppose them." In such a case "one must surely conclude that they are not in keeping with prudence and enlightened zeal." (*Mediator Dei*, 181) More positively, he goes on to state that only those exercises of piety are to be considered wholesome which lead us to the liturgy. "The criterion of this will be the effectiveness of these exercises in making the divine cult loved and spread daily ever more widely, and in making the faithful approach the sacraments with more longing desire, and in obtaining for all things holy due respect and honor." (*Mediator Dei*, 181) Furthermore, the liturgical prayer of the Church is the norm to which all piety must measure up.

> It is necessary that the spirit of the sacred liturgy and its directives should exercise such a salutary influence on them [exercises of piety] that nothing improper be introduced nor anything unworthy of the dignity of the house of God or detrimental to the sacred functions or opposed to solid piety. (*Mediator Dei*, 184)

Private prayer, personal asceticism, and popular devotions, then, have an irreplaceable significance and value in the spiritual life of a true Christian. However, their role in the spiritual life will be assured only insofar as they make us ripe for the liturgy in which our life of grace finds its source and continually renewed nourishment, only insofar as they prolong and carry to fruition what is begun in divine worship: our transformation into Christ.

Concretely this will lead us to center our personal lives around the action of Christ in the Church's liturgical life. Every day he holds out to us the preaching as well as the renewal of his paschal mystery; he intends very specifically to instruct us and to bring us his divine life. We can make no better preparation to receive this grace and make an intelligent application of his mystery to ourselves and our condition than by opening our hearts to it through reflection and meditation on it.

What will be the result? We will be protected from narrowness and pettiness, insured of proportion, harmony and homogeneity in our

102

spiritual life, in that we will have embraced the *whole* Christ. We will become more conscious of the fact that we are members of his mystical body and live its life, and the danger will thereby be lessened of ever divorcing ourselves from the body without which we cannot live. Our apostolate to mankind will also take on a new and proper perspective, for it will be seen as Christ acting in and through us to redeem others. Thus, the liturgy will become what it should be, "the primary and indispensable source of the true Christian spirit." It will truly form us to the image and likeness of the Son of God, and we will accept all the formative influence it wishes to exert on us. It will become for us a vivifying immersion in the mystery of Christ, a sharing in the eternal life of God, a veritable transfiguration through grace to glory, so that "when Christ," our "life, shall appear," then we too "will appear with him in glory." (Col 3,4)

Selected Readings

CHAPTER ONE

Cullman, Oscar, *Early Christian Worship* (London: Student Christian Movement, 1953).

Davis, Charles, *Liturgy and Doctrine* (New York: Sheed and Ward, 1960), Ch. 3, "The History of Salvation," pp. 45-47.

Diekmann, Godfrey L., "Two Approaches to Understanding the Sacraments," *Education and the Liturgy*, Proceedings of the 18th North American Liturgical Week (Elsberry, Missouri: The Liturgical Conference, 1958), pp. 12-27.

Farrell, Walter, *A Companion to the Summa*, Vol. IV: *The Way of Life* (New York: Sheed and Ward, 1942), Ch. 12, "Fruitful Signs of Life," pp. 247-69.

Howell, Clifford, *Of Sacraments and Sacrifice* (Collegeville, Minn.: The Liturgical Press, 1952), Ch. 4, "Of Things Visible and Invisible," pp. 34-44.

Louvel, François, and Louis J. Putz, *Signs of Life* (Notre Dame, Ind.: Fides, 1953).

Roguet, A.-M., *Christ Acts Through Sacraments* (Collegeville, Minn.: The Liturgical Press, 1953). Ch. 2, "Sacred Signs," pp. 18-22.

Scheeben, Matthias, J., *The Mystery of the Church and the Sacraments* (St. Meinrad, Ind.: Grail Publications, 1953).

Schillebeeckx, Edouard, *Le Christ, sacrement de la rencontre de Dieu* (Paris: Cerf, 1960).

———, "The Sacraments: An Encounter with God," *Theology Digest*, 8 (Spring, 1960), 117-21.

Toland, Terrence, "Christian Sacrament: Sign and Experience," *Participation in the Mass*, Proceedings of the 20th North American Liturgical Week (Washington, D.C.: The Liturgical Conference, 1960), pp. 247-53.

CHAPTER TWO

Bouyer, Louis, *The Paschal Mystery* (Chicago: Regnery, 1950).

Casel, Odo, *The Mystery of Christian Worship* (Westminster, Md.: Newman, 1962).

Cooke, Bernard J., "The Sacraments: Encounters with Mystery," *Perspectives*, 6 (November-December, 1961), 7-10.

Davis, Charles, *Liturgy and Doctrine* (New York: Sheed and Ward, 1960), Ch. 2, "The Risen Christ," pp. 25-43; Ch. 5, "Liturgy and Mystery," pp. 75-92.

Durrwell, Francis X., *The Resurrection* (New York: Sheed and Ward, 1960). This basic work, certainly a classic, has served as the foundation of this chapter.

Leeming, Bernard, *Principles of Sacramental Theology* (London: Longmans, 1956).

Lyonnet, Stanislas, "Redemption Through Death and Resurrection," *Worship*, 35 (1961), 281-287; "Redemptive Value of the Resurrection," *Theology Digest*, 8 (Spring, 1960), 89-93.

Miller, John H., "Until He Comes—The Eucharist and the Resurrection," *Thy Kingdom Come—Christian Hope in the Modern World*, Proceedings of the 23rd North American Liturgical Week (Washington, D.C.: The Liturgical Conference, 1963), pp. 39-44.

O'Neill, Colman E., "The Mysteries of Christ and the Sacraments," *The Thomist*, 25 (January, 1962), 1-53.

Plus, Raoul, *In Christ Jesus*, (Westminster, Md.: Newman, 1948).

Prat, Ferdinand, *The Theology of St. Paul*, 2 vols. (Westminster, Md.: Newman, 1946).

Robinson, J. A. T., *The Body. A Study in Pauline Theology* (London: Student Christian Movement, 1952).

Roguet, A.-M., *Christ Acts Through the Sacraments* (Collegeville, Minn.: The Liturgical Press, 1953), Ch. 3, "Signs of Grace," pp. 23-26; Ch. 17, "The Sacraments and the Cross," pp. 157-162.

Stuhlmueller, Carroll, "Teaching the Sacraments from Scripture," *Perspectives,* 5 (September-October, 1960), 17-23.

Thurian, Max, *The Eucharistic Memorial,* 2 vols. Ecumenical Studies in Worship, 7 and 8 (Richmond, Va.: John Knox Press, 1960-61).

Van Roo, William A., "The Resurrection: Instrument of Grace," *Theology Digest,* 8 (Spring, 1960), 94-98.

Wikenhauser, Alfred, *Pauline Mysticism. Christ in the Mystical Teaching of St. Paul* (New York: Herder and Herder, 1960).

CHAPTER THREE

Adam, Karl, *The Christ of Faith* (New York: Pantheon, 1957).

Cerfaux, Lucien, *Christ in the Theology of St. Paul* (New York: Herder and Herder, 1959).

Cody, Aelred, *Heavenly Sanctuary and Liturgy in the Epistle to the Hebrews* (St. Meinrad, Ind.: Grail Publications, 1960).

Cooke, Bernard, "The Sacraments: Encounters with Mystery," *Perspectives,* 6 (November-December, 1961), 7-10.

D'Arcy, Martin, *Christ, Priest and Redeemer* (New York: Macmillan, 1928).

Davis, Charles, *Liturgy and Doctrine* (New York: Sheed and Ward, 1960), Ch. 5, "Liturgy and Mystery," pp. 75-92.

Durrwell, Francis X., *The Resurrection* (New York: Sheed and Ward, 1960). This basic work has served as the foundation of this chapter.

Grossouw, William, *In Christ. A Sketch of the Theology of St. Paul* (Westminster, Md.: Newman, 1952).

Guardini, Romano, *The Lord* (Chicago: Regnery, 1955).

Guitton, Jean, *The Problem of Christ* (New York: Kenedy, 1955).

Héris, Charles, *The Mystery of Christ* (Westminster, Md.: Newman, 1950).

Lécuyer, Joseph, *Le Sacerdoce dans le mystère du Christ* (Paris: Cerf, 1957).

Leeming, Bernard, *Principles of Sacramental Theology* (London: Longmans, 1956).

Marmion, Columba, *Christ the Life of the Soul* (St. Louis: Herder, 1935).

Murchland, Bernard, ed., *God Among Men* (Notre Dame, Ind.: Fides, 1960).

O'Connell, John, "The Priesthood of Christ," *The Priesthood of Christ,* Proceedings of the North American Liturgical Week (Conception, Missouri: The Liturgical Conference, 1952), pp. 19-25.

Prat, Ferdinand, *Jesus Christ, His Life, His Teaching and His Work,* 2 vols. (Milwaukee: Bruce, 1950).

———, *The Theology of St. Paul,* 2 vols. (Westminster, Md., Newman, 1946).

Roguet, A.-M., *Christ Acts Through Sacraments* (Collegeville, Minn.: The Liturgical Press, 1953).

Schillebeeckx, Edouard, *Le Christ, sacrement de la rencontre de Dieu* (Paris: Cerf, 1960).

———, "The Sacraments: An Encounter with God," *Theology Digest,* 8 (Spring, 1960), 117-21.

CHAPTER FOUR

Bobrinskoy, Boris, "Le Saint-Esprit dans la liturgie," *Studia Liturgica,* 1 (1962), 47-59.

Durrwell, Francis X., *The Resurrection* (New York: Sheed and Ward, 1960).

Flicoteaux, Emmanuel, *The Splendor of Pentecost* (Baltimore: Helicon, 1961).

Guillet, Jacques, *Themes of the Bible* (Notre Dame, Ind.: Fides, 1960), Ch. 7, "The Breath of Yahweh," pp. 225-79.

Pope Leo XIII, *Divinum illud,* Encyclical on the Holy Ghost (Rome, 1897), America Press Edition.

Marmion, Columba, *Christ the Life of the Soul* (St. Louis: Herder, 1935).

Pope Pius XII, *Mystici corporis,* Encyclical on the Mystical Body of Christ (Rome, 1943), America Press Edition.

Plus, Raoul, *In Christ Jesus* (Westminster, Md.: Newman, 1948).

Schillebeeckx, Edward, "Ascension and Pentecost," *Worship,* 35 (1961), 336-63.

Swete, Henry B., *The Holy Spirit in the New Testament* (London: Macmillan, 1909).

Vonier, Anscar, "The Spirit and the Bride," In the *Collected Works of Abbot Vonier,* Vol. 2 (Westminster, Md.: Newman, 1952).

CHAPTER FIVE

Adam, Karl, *The Spirit of Catholicism* (Garden City, New York: Doubleday Image Books, 1954).

Bouyer, Louis, *The Word, the Church and the Sacraments in Catholicism and Protestantism* (New York: Desclée, 1961).

Cerfaux, Lucien, *The Church in the Theology of St. Paul* (New York: Herder and Herder, 1957).

Davis, Charles, *Liturgy and Doctrine* (New York: Sheed and Ward, 1960), Ch. 4, "The Church," pp. 59-73.

Durrwell, Francis X., *The Resurrection* (New York: Sheed and Ward, 1960).

Guardini, Romano, *The Church and the Catholic* (New York: Sheed and Ward, 1953).

Leeming, Bernard, *Principles of Sacramental Theology* (London: Longmans, 1956).

Lubac, Henri de, *Catholicism* (New York: Sheed and Ward, 1958).

———, *The Splendour of the Church* (New York: Sheed and Ward, 1956).

Mersch, Emile, *The Whole Christ* (Milwaukee: Bruce, 1938).

———, *The Theology of the Mystical Body* (St. Louis: Herder, 1952).

Murphy, John L., *The Living Christ* (Milwaukee: Bruce, 1952).

Pius XII, *Mystici corporis*, Encyclical on the Mystical Body (Rome, 1943). America Press Edition.

Plus, Raoul, *In Christ Jesus* (Westminster, Md.: Newman, 1948).

Prat, Ferdinand, *The Theology of St. Paul*, 2 vols. (Westminster, Md.: Newman, 1946).

Rahner, Karl, *The Church and the Sacraments*, Quaestiones Disputatae, 9 (New York: Herder and Herder, 1963).

Robinson, J. A. T., *The Body: A Study in Pauline Theology* (London: SCM Press, 1952).

Scheeben, Matthias J., *The Mystery of the Church and the Sacraments* (St. Meinrad, Ind.: Grail Publications, 1953).

Schillebeeckx, Edouard, *Le Christ, sacrement de la rencontre de Dieu* (Paris: Cerf, 1960).

Schlitzer, Albert, *Our Life in Christ*, Vol. 1 (Notre Dame, Ind.: University of Notre Dame Press, 1962).

Semmelroth, Otto, "Towards a Unified Concept of the Church," *Yearbook of Liturgical Studies,* 2 (1961) 85-102.

Sheen, Fulton J., *The Mystical Body of Christ* (New York: Sheed and Ward, 1935).

Vonier, Anscar, *The People of God,* in the *Collected Works of Abott Vonier.* Vol. 2 (Westminster, Md.: Newman, 1952).

CHAPTER SIX

Audet, Lionel, "Notre participation au sacerdoce du Christ," *Laval théologique et philosophique,* 1 (1945), 9-47.

Cerfaux, Lucien, *The Church in the Theology of St. Paul* (New York: Herder and Herder, 1957).

Congar, Yves, "Structure du sacerdoce chrétien," *La Maison-Dieu,* n.27 (1951), 51-85.

————, *Lay People in the Church* (Westminster, Md.: Newman, 1956).

Daniélou, Jean, *The Bible and the Liturgy* (Notre Dame, Ind.: University of Notre Dame Press, 1956).

Davis, H. Francis, "The Priesthood of the Faithful," *Theology Digest,* 1 (Winter, 1953), 49-52.

Héris, Charles, *The Mystery of Christ* (Westminster, Md.: Newman 1950).

Hesburgh, Theodore, *The Theology of Catholic Action. The Sacramental Characters and the Lay Apostolate* (Notre Dame, Ind.: Ave Maria Press, 1946).

Laros, Matthias, *Confirmation in the Modern World* (New York: Sheed and Ward, 1940).

Lécuyer, Joseph, "Essai sur le sacerdoce des fidèles chez les pères," *La Maison-Dieu,* n.27 (1951), 7-50.

————, *Le Sacerdoce dans le mystère du Christ* (Paris: Cerf, 1957).

————, *What Is a Priest?* (New York: Hawthorn, 1959).

Leeming, Bernard, *Principles of Sacramental Theology* (London: Longmans, 1956).

McNamara, Kevin, "Aspects of the Layman's Role in the Mystical Body," *Irish Theological Quarterly,* 25 (1958), 124-43.

O'Connell, John, "The Priesthood of Christ," *The Priesthood of Christ,* Proceedings of the North American Liturgical Week (Conception, Missouri: The Liturgical Conference, 1952), pp. 19-25.

O'Neill, Colman, "The Instrumentality of the Sacramental Character," *Irish Theological Quarterly,* 25 (1958), 262-68.

————, "The Role of the Recipient and Sacramental Signification," *The Thomist*, 21 (1958), 257-301; 508-40.

Palmer, Paul, "Lay Priesthood: Real or Metaphorical?" *Theological Studies*, 8 (1947), 574-613.

————, "Lay Priesthood: Towards a Terminology," *Theological Studies*, 10 (1949), 235-50.

Pius XII, *Mediator Dei*, Encyclical on the Sacred Liturgy (Rome, 1947), America Press edition.

Quinn, J. Richard, "The Sacramental Character as the Key to Understanding the Christian Life," *American Ecclesiastical Review*, 142 (1960), 32-40.

Rea, James, *The Common Priesthood of the Members of the Mystical Body* (Westminster, Md.: Newman, 1947).

Roguet, A-M., "La théologie du charactère et l'incorporation à l'Eglise," *La Maison-Dieu*, n.32 (1952), 74-89.

Scheeben, Matthias J., *The Mystery of the Church and the Sacraments* (St. Meinrad, Ind.: Grail Publications, 1953).

Schillebeeckx, Edouard, *Le Christ, sacrement de la rencontre de Dieu* (Paris: Cerf, 1960).

Schleck, Charles, "The Lay Priesthood and the Mass," *Sciences ecclésiastiques*, 12 (1960), 83-103.

Smedt, Emile-Joseph De, *The Priesthood of the Faithful* (New York: Paulist Press, 1962).

Stevens, Gregory, "Liturgy and Contemplation," *American Ecclesiastical Review*, 142 (1960), 108-15.

Van Camp, J., "The Sacramental Character: Its Role in the Church," *Theology Digest*, 1 (Winter, 1953), 28-32.

CHAPTER SEVEN

Cooke, Bernard, "The Sacraments: Encounters with Mystery," *Perspectives*, 6 (November-December, 1961), 7-10.

Diekmann, Godfrey L., "Two Approaches to the Sacraments," *Education and the Liturgy*, Proceedings of the 18th North American Liturgical Week (Elsberry, Missouri: The Liturgical Conference, 1958), pp. 12-27.

Durrwell, Francis X., *The Resurrection* (New York: Sheed and Ward, 1960).

Gaillard, Jean, "Faith and the Sacraments," *Theology Digest*, 9 (Autumn, 1961), 161-67.

Norris, Frank B., "The Response of Faith in the Sacraments," *The*

Liturgy and Unity in Christ, Proceedings of the 21st North American Liturgical Week (Washington, D. C.: The Liturgical Conference, 1961), pp. 23-27.

Villette, Louis, *Foi et sacrement, I* (Paris: Bloud et Gay, 1959).

CHAPTER EIGHT

The Assisi Papers (Collegeville, Minn.: Liturgical Press, 1957).

Beauduin, Lambert, *Liturgy, the Life of the Church* (Collegeville, Minn.: Liturgical Press, 1929).

Brasó, Gabriel, *Liturgy and Spirituality* (Collegeville, Minn.: Liturgical Press, 1959).

Bouyer, Louis, *Liturgical Piety* (Notre Dame, Ind.: University of Notre Dame Press, 1955).

Casel, Odo, *The Mystery of Christian Worship* (Westminster, Md.: Newman, 1962).

Congar, Yves, *Lay People in the Church* (Westminster, Md.: Newman, 1957).

Coppens, J., "Eucharistie," *Dictionnaire de la Bible, Supplément,* 2 (L. Pirot, ed.; Paris: Letouzey et Ané, 1934), 1146-1215.

Dalmais, Irenée, *Introduction to the Liturgy* (Baltimore: Helicon, 1961).

Davis, Charles, *Liturgy and Doctrine* (New York: Sheed and Ward, 1960).

Diekmann, Godfrey L., *Come, Let Us Worship* (Baltimore: Helicon, 1961).

Ellard, Gerald, *Christian Life and Worship* (Milwaukee: Bruce, 1935).

————, *Men at Work and Worship* (New York: Macmillan, 1940).

————, *The Mass of the Future* (Milwaukee: Bruce, 1948).

Flynn, V., "The Sacramentals of the Church," *American Ecclesiastical Review* 141 (1959), 294-300.

Guardini, Romano, *The Spirit of the Liturgy* (New York: Sheed and Ward, 1954).

————, *Meditations Before Mass* (Westminster, Md.: Newman, 1955).

Hamman, A., *Early Christian Prayers* (Chicago: Regnery, 1961).

Hellriegel, Martin B., *How to Make the Church Year a Living Reality* (St. Louis, 1956).

Howell, Clifford, *Of Sacraments and Sacrifice* (Collegeville, Minn.: Liturgical Press, 1952).

———, *Preparing for Easter* (Collegeville, Minn.: Liturgical Press, 1957).

Jenny, Henri, *The Paschal Mystery in the Christian Year* (Notre Dame, Ind.: Fides, 1961).

Jungmann, Josef A., *Liturgical Worship* (New York: Pustet, 1941).

———, *The Eucharistic Prayer* (Notre Dame, Ind.: Fides, 1956).

———, *The Sacrifice of the Church* (Collegeville, Minn.: Liturgical Press, 1956).

———, *Public Worship* (Collegeville, Minn.: Liturgical Press, 1957).

———, *The Mass of the Roman Rite* (New York: Benziger Brothers, 1958).

———, *The Meaning of Sunday* (Notre Dame, Ind.: Fides, 1961).

———, *Pastoral Liturgy* (New York: Herder and Herder, 1962).

Living with the Church (Loveland, Ohio: Grailville Publications, 1950).

Loehr, Aemiliana, *The Year of the Lord* (New York: Kenedy, 1957).

———, *The Great Week* (Westminster, Md.: Newman, 1958).

Miller, John H., *The Relationship Between Liturgical and Private Prayer* (Trier: Author, 1955).

———, "Liturgical and Private Prayer," *American Ecclesiastical Review* 135 (October, 1956), 257-63.

———, "Nature and Definition of the Liturgy," *Theological Studies* 18 (September, 1957), 257-356.

———, *Fundamentals of the Liturgy* (Notre Dame, Ind.: Fides 1960).

———, "Prayer: Public and Private," *Sponsa Regis* 31 (August, 1960), 344-51.

———, "The Mass, Source of the Christian Spirit," *Spiritual Formation and Guidance-Counseling in the CCD Program,* ed. by Joseph B. Collins (Washington, D.C.: The Catholic University Press, 1962), pp. 95-106.

———, "Until He Comes—The Eucharist and the Resurrection," *Thy Kingdom Come—Christian Hope in the Modern World,* Proceedings of the 23rd North American Liturgical Week (Washington, D.C.: The Liturgical Conference, 1963), pp. 39-44.

Marmion, Columba, *Christ in His Mysteries* (St. Louis: Herder, 1939).

Mueller, Therese, *Family Life in Christ* (Collegeville, Minn.: Liturgical Press, 1952).

O'Shea, William, *The Worship of the Church* (Westminster, Md.: Newman, 1957).

Parsch, Pius, *The Church's Year of Grace*, 5 vols. (Collegeville, Minn.: Liturgical Press, 1953-1962).

Perkins, Mary, *The Sacramental Way* (New York: Sheed and Ward, 1948).

Pius X, Motu Proprio: *Tra le sollecitudini* (Rome, 1904).

Pius XII, *Mediator Dei* (Rome, 1947), America Press Edition. *Instruction on Sacred Music and the Liturgy* (Rome, 1958), NCWC Edition.

Quinn, J. Richard, "The Sacramental Character as the Key to Understanding the Christian Life," *American Ecclesiastical Review* 142 (1960), 32-40.

Reinhold, H. A., *The American Parish and the Roman Liturgy* (New York: Macmillan, 1958).

——, *Bringing the Mass to the People* (Baltimore: Helicon, 1960).

Schuster, Ildephonse, *The Sacramentary*, 5 vols. (New York: Benziger, 1924-1930).

Stevens, Gregory, "Liturgy and Contemplation," *American Ecclesiastical Review* 142 (1960), 108-15.

Thurian, Max, *The Eucharistic Memorial*, 2 vols. Ecumenical Studies in Worship, 7 and 8 (Richmond, Va.: John Knox Press, 1960-61).

Vagaggini, Cyprian, *Theological Dimensions of the Liturgy* (Collegeville, Minn.: Liturgical Press, 1959).

Von Hildebrand, Dietrich, *Liturgy and Personality* (New York: Longmans, 1946).

Wesseling, Theodore, *Liturgy and Life* (New York: Pustet, 1941).

ABBREVIATIONS

The Books of the Old and New Testaments

Genesis	Gn	Canticle of Canticles	Ct
Exodus	Ex	Wisdom	Wis
Leviticus	Lv	Sirach (Ecclesiasticus)	Sir
Numbers	Nm	Isaia	Is
Deuteronomy	Dt	Jeremia	Jer
Joshua	Jos	Lamentations	Lam
Judges	Jgs	Baruch	Bar
Ruth	Ru	Ezechiel	Ez
1 Samuel (1 Kings)	1 Sm	Daniel	Dn
2 Samuel (2 Kings)	2 Sm	Osea	Os
1 Kings (3 Kings)	1 Kgs	Joel	Jl
2 Kings (4 Kings)	2 Kgs	Amos	Am
1 Chronicles (Paralipomenon)	1 Chr	Abdia	Abd
2 Chronicles (Paralipomenon)	2 Chr	Jona	Jon
Ezra	Ez	Michea	Mi
Nehemia (2 Ezra)	Neh	Nahum	Na
Tobia	Tb	Habacuc	Hb
Judith	Jdt	Sophonia	So
Esther	Est	Aggai	Ag
Job	Jb	Zacharia	Za
Psalms	Ps(s)	Malachia	Mal
Proverbs	Prv	1 Machabees	1 Mc
Coheleth (Ecclesiastes)	Coh	2 Machabees	2 Mc

In the enumeration of the Psalms, the first number follows the Vulgate, the number within brackets, the Hebrew text.

St. Matthew	Mt	1 Timothy	1 Tim
St. Mark	Mk	2 Timothy	2 Tim
St. Luke	Lk	Titus	Ti
St. John	Jn	Philemon	Phlm
Acts of the Apostles	Ac	Hebrews	Heb
Romans	Rom	St. James	Jas
1 Corinthians	1 Cor	1 St. Peter	1 Pt
2 Corinthians	2 Cor	2 St. Peter	2 Pt
Galatians	Gal	1 St. John	1 Jn
Ephesians	Eph	2 St. John	2 Jn
Philippians	Phil	3 St. John	3 Jn
Colossians	Col	St. Jude	Jude
1 Thessalonians	1 Thes	Apocalypse	Ap
2 Thessalonians	2 Thes		

Apocrypha and Qumrân Material

Henoch	Hen	Testament of the	
Jubilees	Jub	Twelve Patriarchs	Test
Psalms of Solomon	Ps Sol	Manual of Discipline	MD

Other Source Material

Acta Apostolicae Sedis
[Acts of the Apostolic See]   AAS
Ancient Christian Writers,
     ed. J. Quasten and others   ACW
Acta Sanctae Sedis
[Acts of the Holy See]   ASS
Codex Iuris Canonici
[Code of Canon Law]   CIC
Denzinger-Schönmetzer,
     Enchiridion Symbolorum, 32d ed.
     [Handbook of the Creeds]   D
Patrologia, series graeca,
     ed. J. P. Migne   PG
Sacrorum Conciliorum nova
     . . . Collectio   Mansi

Patrologia, series latina,
     ed. J. P. Migne   PL
Summa contra Gentes
     S. Thomae Aquinatis   S.C.G.
Quatuor Libri Sententiarum
     Petri Lombardi [Four Books
     of Opinions]   Sent.
Summa Theologiae
     S. Thomae Aquinatis   S.Th.
Supplementum tertiae partis Summae
     Theologiae (Ottawa ed. 1941)
          Suppl.
The Church Teaches,
     ed. J. Clarkson and others   TCT

INDEX

A

Abraham, heirs of, 19
Adoptive sonship, 2, 16, 17, 18, 19, 34, 37-39, 48, 88, 89
Advent, 97, 98, 99
Albert the Great, Saint, 21
Altar, 85
Altar boys, 84
Ambrose of Milan, Saint, 35, 99
Amerr, 84
Ascension, feast of, 96
Augustine, Saint, 21, 39, 47, 57, 59, 77, 88

B

Baptism, 19, 22, 23, 38, 43, 47, 53, 55, 56, 57, 58, 60, 61, 69, 70, 71, 72, 79, 82, 83, 87, 94, 95
Berakah, 86
Birthdays of martyrs, 99
Blessings, 78
Body, semitic concept of, 20, 21
Bread, 11, 23, 31, 65, 72-73, 85, 87, 89
Breaking of bread, 85

C

Canon, 84, 85, 87
Catechumenate, 95
Choir, 84
Christ
  as first-fruits, first-born, 18
  his blood, 23, 30, 35, 80
  his wounds, 30
  as priest, 26-31, 50, 51, 57-60, 78-82
  as sacrament, 5, 8, 10, 11, 17, 25, 60, 76, 87, 92

Christmas, 97, 98
Church, 3, 11, 21, 22, 25, 31, 38, 39, 40-48, 57, 58, 59, 60, 61, 68, 69, 70, 73, 74, 78, 79, 80, 81, 82, 83, 84, 88, 89, 91, 92, 93, 95, 96, 97, 100, 101, 102
Church as sacrament, 45, 74
Circumcision, 55, 56
Communion, 48, 85-88
Confirmation, 24, 33, 38, 47, 53, 60, 61, 79
Corpus Christi, 90
Council of Chalcedon (451), 10
Council of Ephesus (431), 100
Council of Trent (1547), 53
Council of the Vatican II (1962), 83
Cyprian of Carthage, Saint, 35, 48
Cyril of Jerusalem, Saint, 38, 53, 54, 55, 56

D

Divinum illud, 47
Donatist heresy, 57

E

Easter, 94-96
Efficacy of sacraments, 22-25, 26-28, 31, 33, 37, 38, 39, 45, 47, 48, 49, 59, 60, 61, 62, 63, 70-74
Elohim, 7
Epiphany, 98
Eucharist, 21, 23, 39, 47, 72, 73, 79, 80, 85-90, 93, 94, 95
Exodus, 7, 86
Exsultet, 94
Extreme Unction, 24-25, 79

F

Faith, 1, 3, 25
  of the Church, 74
  as a "coming to Christ," 65-66
  object of, 63-65
  product of the paschal mystery, 65-67
  and sacraments, 62-74, 75
  social nature of, 68-70
Fall, 13
Family meal, 86-89
Feast, notion of, 91-94
Flesh, 14, 18-21, 30, 90
Friendship, 6, 65, 76, 77, 86

G

Gloria, 99
Good Friday, 94
Gregory I, Pope, 98

H

Habûrah, 86-87
Haggadah, 86
Hippolytus, 35
Holy Orders, 3, 24, 38, 53, 60, 79
Holy Spirit, 9, 11, 15, 16, 17, 18, 19, 20,
    21, 24, 32-39, 42, 43, 46, 47, 49,
    52, 54, 55, 56, 60, 65, 66, 67, 70,
    71, 72, 74, 78, 91, 94, 95, 96, 97,
    100
Holy Week, 94-95
Hypostatic union, 6

I

In Christ Jesus, 17-21
Incarnation, 2-11, 13, 14, 28, 29, 56, 60,
    79
Institution of sacraments, 27, 78
Instruction on Sacred Music and Liturgy
    (1958), 83
Irenaeus, Saint, 35
Isidore of Seville, Saint, 39

J

Jerome, Saint, 35
John Chrysostom, Saint, 21, 54

L

Laity, 81, 82
Lent, 95
  of St. Martin, 97
Leo the Great, Pope, 31, 94, 96
Leo XIII, Pope, 47
Liturgical Year, 90-103
Liturgy, 75-103
Lord's Prayer, 88
Lord's Supper, 85

M

Magic, 70, 76
Marriage, 11, 24, 43, 79
Martin, feast of Saint (Nov. 11), 97
Martyrs, feasts of, 99
Mary, Blessed Virgin, 99, 100
Mass, 84-90
  of catechumens, 87
  participation in, 60, 81-84
Meal, sacred, 85-90, 94
Mediator, 26, 83
Mediator Dei, 80, 81, 93, 101, 102
Melchisedech, 28, 29
Memorial, 86-87, 89, 90, 92, 93
Mental prayer, 101, 102
Mersch, Emile, 43
Mysteries of Christ's life in the Liturgical
    Year, 93
Mystical Body, 19-22, 25, 33, 40-48, 60,
    68-70, 71, 79, 81, 82, 83, 84, 88,
    89, 99, 102
Mystici corporis, 33, 45-47

N

Name of Jesus, 79-81
Nicene Creed, 33, 37

O

Offertory, 85, 88
Origen, 35

P

Palm Sunday, 94
Parousía, 98

Participation, active, 81-84
Paschal candle, 94
Paschal mystery and faith, 63-67
Paschal mystery
  and Christ's priesthood, 26-31
  and Holy Spirit, 32-39
  and faith, 65-67
  in the liturgy, 77-79, 84, 86-89, 91-93, 99, 100, 102
  and the sacraments, 12-25, 73, 74
Paschal time, 95
Passion, 14-17, 25, 30, 36, 89, 90
Passover, 54, 85-87
Penance, 24, 38, 47-48, 79, 95
Pentecost, 34, 96, 97
People of God, 8, 48, 49, 50, 81, 87, 89
Permanence of redemptive act, 17, 22, 26-31
Peter Lombard, 77
Pius X, Saint, 83
Pius XII, Pope, 32, 45, 46, 80, 81, 93, 101, 102
Prayer, private, 101-102
Preface-canon, 84, 85, 86
Priesthood, 3, 26-31, 49-61, 62, 68, 78-83, 92, 93
  of laity, 49-61, 81-84
Proclaim the death of the Lord, 23, 24, 90
Proclamation of Word of God, 92
Prodigal son, 13, 16, 17, 47-48

R

Rahner, Karl, 45
Resurrection, 12-25, 27-31, 32-39, 44, 63-67, 71, 74, 88-90, 93-94, 99, 100
Revelation, 1-3, 101
Rufinus, 35

S

Sacramental character, 49-61, 81-84
Sacramental grace, 11, 21-25, 57, 58, 59, 77, 88, 89, 90
Sacramentals, 77-79, 92-93, 95, 100, 101
Sacraments
  as actions of Christ, 3, 11, 26-31, 59, 60, 61
  and the Church, 40-48, 59-61, 73-74
  and faith, 62-74
  and Holy Spirit, 32-39, 46-47, 49, 54, 55

Sacraments (*Cont.*):
  and incarnation, 2-11, 56, 60, 79
  and paschal mystery, 12-25, 73, 74
  and priesthood, 3, 49-61
Sacrifice, 14, 25, 27, 28, 29, 30, 31, 51, 58, 59, 77, 80, 86, 88, 89, 90, 93, 94
Saints, feasts of, 99-100
Salvation-history, 2, 7
Sanctus, 84
Seal of the covenant, 55-57
Semmelroth, Otto, 45
Sign, 6, 8, 9, 10, 11, 25, 27, 28, 31, 47, 55, 56, 59, 60, 73, 75, 77, 78, 79, 82, 83, 84, 87, 89
Social nature of
  faith, 68-70
  liturgy, 81-84, 88, 89, 93, 95, 101, 102
  sacraments, 45-48
Solidarity between Christ and Christians, 14, 15, 16, 17, 18, 19, 20, 21, 22, 23, 24, 25, 27, 30, 31, 37, 38, 39, 40-48
Sphragis, 53-56
Spiritual life, 2, 3, 59, 62, 65, 66, 72, 90, 91, 93, 100-103
Symbolism, 23, 83, 85, 86

T

Tabernacles, feast of, 34-35
Te Deum, 99
Teleiōsis, 51
Theodore of Mopsuestia, 53, 54
Theology, 1-3, 5
Thomas Aquinas, Saint, 46, 57, 58, 59, 76, 79, 90
Through our Lord Jesus Christ, 81
Time, Christian meaning of, 91
Tra le sollecitudini, 83

V

Veiling of images, 95

W

Water, 11, 31, 35, 37
Wine, 11, 31, 85, 90
Worship, 75-103

Z

Zeal, 70, 74